THE
COMMON SENSE
OF
MONEY AND INVESTMENTS

Wiley Investment Classics

THE
COMMON SENSE
OF
MONEY AND INVESTMENTS

Merryle Stanley Rukeyser

Financial Editor, New York *Evening Journal*;
Associate in Journalism, Columbia University;
formerly Financial and Business Editor,
New York *Tribune* and *Vanity Fair*

John Wiley & Sons, Inc.
New York • Chichester • Weinheim • Brisbane • Singapore • Toronto

To my mother

This book is printed on acid-free paper. ∞

Copyright © 1924, 1999 by Simon & Schuster (original pub).
All rights reserved.

Published by John Wiley & Sons, Inc.
Published simultaneously in Canada.

This publication is designed to provide accurate and authoritative
information in regard to the subject matter covered. It is sold with the
understanding that the publisher is not engaged in rendering professional
services. If professional advice or other expert assistance is required, the
services of a competent professional person should be sought.

Library of Congress Cataloging-in-Publication Data:

Rukeyser, Merryle Stanley, 1897–1988.
     The common sense of money and investments / by Merryle Stanley
Rukeyser.
          p.   cm. — (Wiley investment classics)
     Includes index.
     Originally published: New York : Simon & Schuster, 1924.
     ISBN 0-471-33212-7 (cloth : alk. paper). — ISBN 0-471-33213-5
(pbk. : alk. paper)
     1. Investments. 2. Finance, Personal. I. Title. II. Series.
HG4521.R8   1999
332.6—dc21   99-30159

Printed in the United States of America
10 9 8 7 6 5 4 3 2 1

FOREWORD

The most remarkable thing about this classic book—other than that its author was, as the original introduction pointed out, "the first to set down in book form the problems of the inexperienced small investor in intangibles, and the solution of these problems"—is how surprisingly well the book's basic advice stands up three quarters of a century after its initial publication. In a world where ridiculously hyped tomes promising instant financial euphoria for ordinary citizens now vie with counsel on health and sex in every bookstore, old-fashioned common sense still takes the prize. Most of the would-be gurus, not to mention their customers, would have been better off if they had read this one first.

This is not just my judgment as the second of four sons of the author. Serendipitously, while I was getting ready to write this Foreword at the behest of Mina Samuels, a gracious editor at John Wiley & Sons, Inc., out of the blue came a copy of the book sent along by my friend Warren Buffett, the most celebrated and successful investor of the late twentieth century. "Dear Lou," he wrote. "The enclosed was found in an estate sale. Evidently the advice in it worked, since the owner left a large estate. I skimmed it and found it to be a first-class book that stands the test of time."

And so it does. When Merryle Rukeyser wrote in 1924, there was no Internet, no listed options trading, no computer-guided program selling. But the enduring themes of hustle and fraud, surefire get-rich-quick schemes, and cynical disdain for the problems of inexperienced individual investors were all in place and make the book's sane and savvy perspective surprisingly relevant. Checked out the blind advice on a web site lately? Read here about the deliberate misdirection of "unscrupulous stock vendors." Excited by some "hot tip" on cable TV? Read here why "most tips are likely to be misleading. Following them blindly is virtually a certain road to financial ruin." Tempted by the prospect of a "safe speculation"? Read here why that's like looking for "dry water, or still motion." Seduced by a one-two-three prescription for turning yourself into a billionaire CEO? Read here about the pitfalls in "the theory that, if everyone works diligently enough, 110 million bank presidencies will open up." What Alphonse Karr wrote precisely 75 years before this book was published remains stunningly valid 75 years later: *"Plus ça change, plus c'est la même chose."* The tools may work faster now, but the essential wisdom has not altered.

Even some of the political and social commentary reads as if it were taken from today's newspapers. Is a mass population that formerly found finance remote and inexplicable suddenly turning into a nation of investors? That's what they thought in 1924, too. Is it a phenomenon of the post-Communist era to discern currency troubles beyond the Volga? Read here about "the Russian rouble" leaping "madly toward worthlessness." Is it a new idea to talk about "socially responsible" investing? Read here the limits prescribed by a deep thinker of the day on precisely where it's okay, and not okay, for "Socialists and Radicals" to practice capitalism. Even one of the most notable prospects of the new millennium, a shift in political power occasioned by the burgeoning numbers of private individual investors, is foreshadowed by the post-World War I discovery that a fellow who owns a few stocks and bonds is less likely to succumb to "blind intemperate hatred" of corporations.

And speaking of enduring wisdom, what may most surprise modern-day readers of this book, who make the necessary adjustments for inflation and greater longevity, will be that the author himself was just 27 years old—and single. His credits were already imposing. Merryle Rukeyser was the boy wonder of financial journalism, having become financial editor of the New

Foreword

York *Tribune* at the age of 23. By then he was also teaching financial journalism part-time at Columbia University, as he did for seventeen years. When the book was published, he had moved to the New York *Evening Journal;* he subsequently spent more than three decades as a nationally syndicated newspaper columnist, adding numerous other writing and lecture achievements along the way. As television viewers will remember, he had a fresh burst of celebrity in the final years before his death in December 1988, thirteen days short of his ninety-second birthday.

When I first introduced him as my special guest on *Wall $treet Week with Louis Rukeyser* in 1984, we had already been on the air for fourteen years, and I figured that by then, viewers could count on me not just to be showing them home movies during prime time. The reaction was overwhelming—"Where have you been hiding this guy?"—and he quickly became the most popular guest in our history: the runaway winner when we later asked viewers for nominations to our Hall of Fame. As he showed each time he appeared, he was able to combine good humor and the insights gained in seven decades of watching the American financial scene with a humility rarely found on Wall Street. Once, for example, I asked him whether the current situation reminded him of any of the markets of the past. Ask that question of any routine financial type, and you'll immediately be told glibly and authoritatively that it is exactly like February 1962 or October 1974 or August 1987, or whatever. My father's answer was characteristically wiser: although there were certain similarities to markets of the past, which he delineated, we had never previously had the sustained inflation from which we were then recovering, and that, therefore, made it necessary to assess current conditions and prospects in a new light. "The only thing that's constant," he told me during another television appearance, "is human nature and human psychology, and we still are subject to the madness of crowds." To get a head start in avoiding such madness, read on.

LOUIS RUKEYSER

ACKNOWLEDGMENTS

To the publishers of the New York *Evening Journal,* the New York *Tribune, Vanity Fair,* and the *Medical Review of Reviews,* the author is indebted for permission to reprint articles of his which appeared in those publications. He received valuable editorial assistance from J. I. Bogen, who did research work in connection with several of the chapters. The author is also indebted to innumerable bankers, brokers, and corporation officials for information furnished over a period of years. He is also grateful to readers of publications of which he has been financial editor for illuminating letters which helped to reveal the financial problems of ordinary individuals, and to hundreds of students before whom he has lectured at Columbia University for their ingenuity in raising questions with which this book deals.

CONTENTS

PART I. WHY INVEST?—A COMMON SENSE PROBLEM

[ix]

Contents

PART II. DONT'S FOR INVESTORS—AND A FEW AFFIRMATIONS

[x]

Contents

[xi]

Contents

[xii]

Contents

APPENDIX

INTRODUCTION

by

LAWRENCE CHAMBERLAIN

Chairman, Education Committee, Investment Bankers
Association of America

"Of the making of books there is no end": this is
getting to be true even of books on matters connected
with American investment. The ebullition of the
World War has upheaved a new set of investment
problems in this country, as well as elsewhere, that
require solution. Not the least among them is the
problem of helping the Liberty bond buyer to maintain his hold on this, to him, newly realized kind of
wealth, and to assist him, as he progresses in prosperity, to broaden his grip on securities by intro-
ducing him to forms of intangible wealth other than
Liberty bonds.

There are, perhaps, few not engaged in the business of distributing securities who realize the fact
that prior to the War the great majority of American
citizens had no personal acquaintance with bonds and

[xv]

stocks and no ownership in them; that subsequent to
the War the converse is equally true. A tremendous
step forward is made in economic and financial
education when Tom, Dick, and Harry, by the physical possession of pieces of paper, realize the conveniences and other values peculiar to intangible
wealth. The most direct contact with "intangibles"
that most of these people have is through the financial
columns of the daily press. The most direct personal
contact, therefore, possible to them is with the
financial editor, particularly of the metropolitan
dailies. These men, rather than the investment
bankers, have sensitive fingers on the pulses of the
small investors. They more than any others, through
the medium of countless letters addressed to them by
their readers, understand the experiences, the mis-
fortunes, and the aspirations of those who are seeking
to prosper through the ownership of small sums invested in securities.

It is, therefore, very appropriate that one of these
financial editors, Mr. Merryle Stanley Rukeyser, of
the *New York Evening Journal,* should be the first to
set down in book form the problems of the inexperienced small investor in intangibles, and the solution
of these problems. In doing this Mr. Rukeyser is
not only rendering a highly important service to a
very large part of the community which hitherto has

been without a recognized and generally known source of help and guidance, but he is also making a notable contribution of literature on the subject of how the inexperienced investor may best be safeguarded against predatory concerns selling worthless or fraudulent securities. He joins the increasing number of those who are making it plain that in the long run investment education is the only safeguard against the sale of fraudulent securities, and that so called Blue Sky legislation, as distinguished from the sincere enforcement of penal laws, already spread freely on the statute books, is merely political pap, and an encumbrance to the efficient and economical raising of investment capital through the distribution of securities.

These are the more important reasons why I welcome this contribution of homespun truths to the growing literature of investment.

CHAPTER I

A COMMON SENSE VIEW OF MONEY

Introductory: The Human Significance of Finance.

The butcher has more meat in his shop than he himself can consume, and the brewer and the baker would each of them be willing to purchase a part of it.   But they have nothing to offer in exchange, except the different productions in their respective trades, and the butcher is already provided with all the bread and beer which he has immediate occasion of. . . . In order to avoid the inconveniency of such situations, every prudent man in every period of society, after the first establishment of the division of labor, must naturally have at all times by him, besides the peculiar produce of his own industry, a certain quantity of some one commodity or other, such as he imagined few people would be likely to refuse in exchange for the produce of their industry.—ADAM SMITH.

THIS book is intended as an introduction to the whole subject of finance, as it affects the everyday problems of the ordinary man or woman.   It has been conceived as a means of bridging the gap between a textbook on economics and a bond circular; a link between an abstract thesis and the importunings of a stock salesman.

[1]

It makes no pretense at contributing new theories to be tested at the round tables of specialists. It is rather an effort to tell the layman the essentials of those financial problems which he must inevitably face in his own struggle to maintain a roof over his head, to get clothing to cover his nakedness, and food for his physical nourishment. In attempting to strip the mystery from investment and speculation, from a common-sense standpoint, it goes a step further, and indicates how present labor may in part be conserved for future uses.

The author, who received in the course of three years more than 30,000 inquiries about practical financial questions from newspaper and magazine readers, was frequently called upon to suggest useful books. He has done so freely, having compiled a list of works which seem admirable for sundry needs. However, he has frequently felt and often been told that there was a need for a single volume which would sum up the common sense essence of the entire subject, briefly and within two covers.

This volume has been conceived from the human standpoint. It deals with man's material requirements primarily. Stocks, and bonds, and banks, instead of being the subject of discussion, are looked upon merely as instruments which serve specific human needs. Virtually every man or woman is concerned

[2]

with money making or spending, or saving, and this book aims to deal suggestively with universal needs.

It is written under no delusion that man is an economic creature. The economic activities of a human being constitute only one aspect of life. The intention of the author is not to stress unduly the human significance of money getting and using. The book is written rather in the belief that the artist, the housewife, the physician, and the minister will be freer to attain their spiritual objectives, if the bread and butter side of life is clearly understood and definitely planned. Money making and saving is infinitely more enslaving when manipulated by an ignorant bungler than by one who understands the science of finance in its practical aspects and reacts almost automatically to a program of consistent work, intelligent spending, and systematic saving.

Before the war, corporation finance was of interest to the Four Hundred. Now it is the concern of the Four Million. Prior to 1914, for example, in all the states and territories of the United States there were approximately 400,000 bondholders—a negligible group from the criterion of numbers. In 1917, having joined the European fray and needing larger loans than had ever been arranged since man became a two-legged animal, the United States Treasury went to every home in quest of funds. Millionaires alone could not supply the financial sinews of war. The floating of Liberty bonds concerned not merely Wall Street, but Main Street and all the back alleys, too, in every city and hamlet. Government bonds went to 20,000,000 buyers, and the masses for the first time participated in the strange adventure of coupon-clipping and learned of the weird magic of compound interest.

Having acquired a first hand knowledge of securities, the average man has never since stepped out of the money market. Soon after the government had sold the highest-grade issues to patriotic millions, schemers, charlatans, and fakers began a heinous career of exchanging Liberty bonds for securities that promised infinitely more but yielded little or nothing.

Secretary of the Treasury Mellon recently lent his authority to the oft-repeated estimate that $1,000,-000,000 a year is frittered away by the American public in worthless or questionable securities. To the individual, such deception frequently entails genuine tragedy—a laudable ambition, such as education of one's children, unrealized. To the community, it represents the loss that comes from false and unproductive activities and from misdirected capital. Without a background of elementary financial knowledge, the small investor is like a child wander-

[4]

ing through a tangled forest, trusting blindly to luck.

In attempting to reveal in the simple language of the ordinary man and woman the seeming mysteries and obscurities of money and investment, the author hopes not to convert high minded folk to an excessive interest in materialism, but wishes to suggest a workable technique that will be helpful to the pursuer of beauty, the dreamer of dreams, as well as to the man of affairs. Baser men, to whom acquisition of goods and their symbols, is the sum total of life, already know the tricks of the market-place. And since humanity's friends cannot escape the obligation to supply the elementary requirements and comforts for their families, it is hoped that the hints in this volume will help them better to gauge the meaning and opportunities of modern business.

Business and finance can be treated from various points of view—their social utility, their effect on modern art and philosophy, on politics, on the welfare of the individual. This book is concerned with the specific operations by which the individual can employ the legitimate devices of present-day economic machinery best to attain the prerequisites of physical well-being. To use the analogy of the automobile, the book does not raise the question whether the motor car is the best conceivable means of locomotion; it tells the reader how to run the car.

CHAPTER II

WHEN TO ENJOY THE FRUITS OF YOUR LABOR

Choice between spending and saving; Why invest? Dangers of excessive thrift.

It is not a wise economy which tends to lower the vitality of any member of the family in order that provision may be made for the future.—MARY WILCOX BROWN.

There is not anything in this world more talked of, and less understood, than the business of a happy life. It is every man's wish and design. We live, however, in a blind and eager pursuit of it; and the more haste we make in a wrong way, the farther we are from our journey's end.— SENECA.

No salaried man ever grew rich from salary alone. Only by saving and wisely investing can he become independent of his salary. Money will work. It does the business of the world. It is a question whether you will set it to work for you or blow it in to work for the other fellow.—THOMAS E. SAUNDERS.

But if any provide not for his own, and especially for those of his own house, he hath denied the faith, and is worse than an infidel.—TIMOTHY.

"EAT, drink and be merry," says the epicure, "for to-morrow you die." Such is the philosophy of thrift-

[6]

lessness—the dogma of improvidence. Freed from the overstimulus of artificial merriment, the individual remembers that to-morrow he lives, or at least his obligations live after him.

A deliberate scheme of dissipating one's energies and one's resources currently leads inevitably to financial ruin. Thrift is a scheme by which a small portion of the fruits of one's current labor are diverted for future happiness or well-being. Intelligent saving gives the future a lien on an individual's current productivity. It is a device for tying to-morrow to to-day.

Investment, entailing the placing of thrift funds in channels that will assure reasonable return on moneys employed, entails a quest for deferred happiness. It involves self-denial. It means negativing impulses to use one's purchasing power at present in order that it may be employed at some later day.

Investment presupposes faith—a belief that society will continue present economic arrangements so that benefits currently foregone may be enjoyed in the future. Investment involves confidence in those corporations or governments to whom thrift funds are entrusted for profitable use. Investment in contracts in the form of mortgages or bonds by which borrowers agree to pay back a specified sum at a

[7]

given date signifies an assumption that the money standards in which such agreements are expressed are stable.

Parenthetically, it may be said that no perfect money standards have yet been evolved. Unfortunately financial yardsticks themselves fluctuate and in sundry subtle ways thwart the impulses of all except the most canny investors. As Professor Irving Fisher indicates in a symposium of the views of experts called, "How to Invest when Prices are Rising":

"The investor is one who makes a present sacrifice in order to gain a future return. If prices rise between the present sacrifice and the future return, the fact is bound to influence the results. If the promised return is a definite sum of money, the rise of prices means that the purchasing power of this money will be curtailed. In a general way, during the recent decade and a half of upward prices, it is the bondholder who has lost and the stockholder who has gained."

Since this observation was made by the Yale professor, economic forces have turned in the reverse direction. When commodity prices declined, the purchasing power of money rose and bondholders fared relatively far better than stockholders.

Where currencies leap madly toward worthlessness, as in the case of the German mark and the Russian rouble, contracts—such as life insurance, bonds and mortgages—expressed in terms of those currencies shrink in real value almost to the vanishing point. John Maynard Keynes, the English economist and critic, treats the effect of change in the value of money in investments in his book on "Monetary Reform."

"The effect of the War and of the monetary policy which has accompanied and followed it," he says, "has been to take away a large part of the real value of the possessions of the upper classes. The loss has been so rapid and so intermixed in the time of its occurrence with other worse losses that its full measure is not separately apparent. But it has effected, nevertheless, a far reaching change in the relative position of different classes. Throughout the Continent the pre-war savings of the middle class, so far as they were invested in bonds, mortgages, or bank deposits, have been largely or entirely wiped out. Nor can it be doubted that this experience must modify social psychology towards the practice of saving and investment. What was deemed most secure has proved least so. He who neither spent nor speculated, who made proper provision for his family, who sang hymns to security and observed most straitly the morals of the edified and the respectable injunctions of the worldly wise—he, indeed, who gave fewest pledges to fortune has yet suffered her heaviest visitations.

"What moral for our present purpose should we draw from this? Chiefly, I think, that it is not safe or fair to combine the social organization developed during the nineteenth century (and still retained) with a *laisser-faire* policy towards the value of money. It is not true that our former arrangements have worked well. If we are to continue to draw the voluntary saving of the community into investment, we must make it a prime object of deliberate state policy that the standard of value in terms of which they are expressed, should be kept stable; adjusting in other ways (calculated to touch all forms of wealth equally and not concentrated on the relatively helpless investors) the redistribution of national wealth, if, in course of time, the laws of inheritance and the rate of accumulation have drained too great a proportion of the income of the active classes into the spending control of the inactive. . . .

"The individualistic capitalism of to-day, precisely because it entrusts saving to the individual investor and production to the individual employer presumes a stable measuring rod of value and cannot be efficient—perhaps cannot survive—without one."

Consider the seemingly provident German who

twenty years ago took out an endowment policy worth the equivalent of $10,000. To-day, for all his self-denial he receives a small fraction of a cent. This appears to warrant a cynical attitude toward all the beckonings of thrift. Such a reaction is natural, yet not wise. Because peasant homes, built with great tenderness and love throughout Northern France, were battered down to mere pulp by Teuton guns, it does not follow that we in America should shrink from the impulse to construct new and better homes. Similarly, the effacement of the mark and the rouble investment—and the watering of investments in francs and lire and other depreciated currencies—should not drive Americans to the conclusion that no constructive financial program is likely to bring to the individual the benefits that he is searching for. As a matter of fact, the dollar, though it is an imperfect standard of value, has stood up better during the abnormal years of war and reconstruction than any other unit of currency in the world.

A more stable currency than any that has yet been evolved, the ideal formulated by Fisher, Keynes, and other economists, would make the rôle of the investor infinitely more simple and certain. It would assure him that a dollar invested to-day would have the same purchasing power in the future.

Under present conditions, to avoid all losses from

[11]

fluctuating conditions, the investor must be agile indeed, knowing when to shift from stocks to bonds and when to transfer his savings from long term to short term securities.[1] Perfectionists are doomed to disappointment whenever the human element, which is subject to error, enters. In the sphere of investments, for example, there is no absolute safety; safety is relative and the discriminating and well-advised can find in these approximations to theoretical ideals the means of attaining their legitimate objectives.[2]

Why invest?

First, because by investing or entrusting funds in a productive enterprise or government, an individual increases his total income by adding the return on his securities to current earnings based on his own mental or physical labor.

Moreover, by putting his surplus earnings to work, the individual is facilitating an increase in national productivity and is thus enlarging the social income, on which society draws to finance its commonplace requirements and its noblest aspirations. The socially desirable man is not the easy spender, but the individual who doles out his funds with intelligent discrimination, saving some and converting his thrift

---

[1] See Chap. XI on "When to Switch from Stocks to Bonds."
[2] See Chap. III on "The Legitimate Objectives of Thrift."

funds into capital in the form of productive machinery represented by corporate securities.

Investment connects the individual to the throbbing economic activity of the nation. It gives him the thrill of participation in digging of tunnels through great mountains, the spanning of rivers, the fertilization of arid fields, and the manufacture of a variety of new and useful products which assure a rising standard of living for the great masses of his fellow men.

Under the present capitalistic organization of society, the accumulation of capital is the task and the duty of the individual. Unless such steady accumulation goes on, the great development of factories and plants and the erection of huge buildings and offices must cease. In a socialistic society, presumably the state would arbitrarily and automatically endeavor to set aside a portion of the current social income for conversion into a capital fund. Individual thrift now accomplishes that result.

For social purposes, it is conceivable that individuals might save too large a portion of their income and spend relatively too little.

J. A. Hobson, the British economist, in his new book on "The Economics of Unemployment" says, "Now if you hold, as seems to be the case, that a depression is due to, or testifies to, the existence

[13]

of an excess of producing power and a corresponding deficiency of consuming power, we can only mean that somehow or other there has been oversaving or underspending on the part of industrial society in the sense that more non-consumable, i. e., capital, goods have been created than have been capable of being properly utilized for the supply of future consumption. This is not a theory or an explanation, but rather a description of the actual facts. At a time of depression large bodies of capital stand idle, together with the labor and business ability that could operate them. They simply represent a surplus or excess of former savings which cannot get used without delay and waste for the productive end for which they were designed.

". . . This thesis may be presented in the following manner:

"Just as waste of productive power admittedly occurs by misapplication of capital, skill, and labor, as between one trade and another, or one area of investment and another (too much applied here, too little there) so income as a whole may be wastefully applied as between purchase of commodities and purchase of new capital goods."

There are, of course, natural correctives which tend to prevent over-investment by the social group and also under-investment. These adjustments are never perfect, but if they should ever fail to operate with some measure of success, an economic society would wither and decay. For example, when a disproportionately large amount is being saved, the effect is a fall in the return on capital which in turn tends to discourage investment. On the other hand, when an unduly small amount is being accumulated, the rate of return on capital funds steadily rises and thus makes saving or investment more attractive and tends to induce marginal individuals who would not have saved for a four per cent return to accumulate funds under the lure of a seven per cent return, for example.

Apart from the social aspects of this question, the individual faces dangers of excessive thrift. For example, a father who denies his children an ample education and perhaps even sufficiently nourishing food and an attractive home life so that he can enjoy the strange thrill of watching his pile of gold grow faster than his income really warrants is pursuing an unwise course. The man who denies himself good books, visits to the theater or the opera, travel and a vacation once a year, if his means permit, so that he can accumulate capital faster than his income justifies, is not really thrifty in a higher sense of the word. Money is purchasing power and the true use of money is neglected by the miserly individual whose passion in life is hoarding funds.

But for every miser there are tens of thousands of spendthrifts—individuals who in their senseless whirl of self-gratification dissipate their economic energies, setting up no reserves against the inevitable wearing out of their physical machines, against the day of sickness or premature death.

No universal rules as to the precise amount that an individual should save can be formulated. Rents, for example, are a larger item in the city than in the country. The man with a wife and five children needs a different formula than the bachelor. The principles by which an individual can formulate his own program, however, are discussed in Chapter 28, (Avoiding Bankruptcy in the Pantry.)

Good advice for the average man would be: Save regularly and for definite purposes.[3]

Spend wisely and in accordance with a well considered plan. Make the accumulation of a thrift fund an important incident in your life but one subordinate to the larger problem of living well and usefully.

[3] See Chap. III on "The Legitimate Objectives of Thrift."

CHAPTER III

LEGITIMATE OBJECTIVES OF THRIFT

Human Goals for the individual who saves.

The greatest secret of success in life is to be ready when your opportunity comes.—DISRAELI.

The spirit of thrift does not involve stinginess, which is an abuse of thrift, nor does it require that each item of savings should be a financial investment. The money that is spent in the education of oneself or of one's family, in travel, in music, in art, or in helpfulness to others, if it brings real returns in personal development or in a better understanding of the world we live in, is in accordance with the spirit of thrift.—DAVID STARR JORDAN.

IT is no job of the economist to make out a respectable case for stinginess.

The miser is by no means the ideal of intelligent thrift.

A well ordered economic life entails a wise balance between saving and spending. No single formula can fit the requirements of every case. Extravagance is a relative term. The records of the divorce courts eloquently illustrate this principle. The plea is frequently being made that a divorced woman is unable to live according to the standards to which she is accustomed on $25,000, $50,000, or even $100,000 a year, as the case may be. And yet on another street, a family of seven may be getting a full measure of happiness and comfort on an income of $3,500 a year.

To some a used Ford car would seem a wasteful luxury. To others, two automobiles for every member of the family seem an utter necessity.

In a strict sense, every expenditure beyond those needed to keep the biological processes of metabolism going entails the buying of luxuries. But, in a nation with a relatively high average standard of living, the plain citizen has come to expect more out of life than a minimum of essential food, a roof to protect him from inclemencies of the weather, and clothing to cover his nakedness.

Economic progress, as a matter of fact, is measured by the multiplications of wants. The luxuries of to-day become the necessities of to-morrow. An index of the material welfare of a democratic society is the capacity of the masses to command goods. The limits to consumption bear a close relation to the productive ability of an economic unit.

The sure road to the ideal economic life then lies not in exaggerated self-denial and penury.

[18]

Legitimate Objectives of Thrift

For the individual, saving merely means storing up, instead of exhausting, purchasing power. It entails deferring the satisfactions which come from spending. It involves transferring present claims on society for goods and services into future drafts. It signifies holding a blank check for subsequent use.

Elementary desires and passions conspire to advise, "Spend Now." Likewise every merchant and manufacturer, with every show window and advertisement, contribute to the forces urging the individual to spend his money. The frailties in this direction of the head of the family are frequently intensified by the pleas of other members of the household.

The conventional urgings of investment bankers and of thrift societies are feeble offsets indeed to these more basic appeals. Perhaps that is why most men who pass beyond the years of productivity find themselves impecunious, forced to live upon the charity of relatives or of the community.

Theoretically, the ordinary individual is compensated for the sacrifice of present desires which saving involves by the receipt of interest or dividends on his investment. Moreover, men of larger wealth save because only through the employment of capital are they able to carry out their major business programs and aspirations. Folk of extraordinary wealth are automatic savers, literally unable to spend their current income.

What human goals ought to determine the investment program of the ordinary individual? What objectives are legitimate and justify the sacrifice that saving signifies?

No one can present an exhaustive list, which will include all the infinite varieties of life.

However, a few considerations which are likely to be of general application may be enumerated.

First: The building up of a fund to finance retirement is a common objective of investors. Since the human machine inevitably wears out, each year's income is in part a using up of capital. A part of the annual product should therefore be saved to provide a livelihood after the age of 65—to set an arbitrary age—when one's physical and mental condition no longer permit active full employment.

Each individual, in laying out his personal financial chart, should decide early in life at what age he intends to retire, and should figure out how much needs to be saved each year to create a fund, the interest on which after retirement will meet his financial requirements.

It would be well to figure on making large deposits during the years of maximum productivity between 30 and 45. Fortunately, an individual's requirements after 65 are usually less than earlier in life, because in all likelihood his dependent children will have reached the age of self-support. Funds intended to finance a graceful retirement should be invested in sound securities, entailing only a small degree of speculative risk.

Second: A fund such as the foregoing should be available also to take care of emergencies, such as sickness, operations, unemployment of the head of the family and his dependents, or premature death. Savings might well be supplemented by the carrying of health, accident, and life insurance policies.

Third: An investment structure is frequently planned to provide the means for education and travel, either for the saver or for close relatives. In selecting securities for a fund of this character, it is often well to pick out bonds that will mature approximately at the time the funds will be needed.

Fourth: An investment fund is sometimes created out of savings from salaries of employes who have an ambition later to go into business of their own. Moreover, the small business man will frequently save to finance the future expansion and development of his enterprise. In doing this, he is proceeding along the same lines as the larger corporation which plows back earnings into the property as surplus to pay for improvements and betterments.

[21]

Schooled to some extent in the ways of enterprise, the thrifty business man is usually justified in choosing higher yielding securities which entail a larger degree of risk than the ordinary individual saving for old age, or illness, or other emergencies.

Fifth: Saving enough for a first payment on a home is a common motive in economic life. Similar forces induce thrift to make possible an automobile, a piano, or other high priced article for home use. In all these cases, provision is made for purchase on the partial payment plan, which means that a bulk of the saving must be done after the commodity has been acquired.

Sixth: Prudent men also build up an estate as a reserve against speculative or business mistakes. For example, the reckless professional speculator frequently buys an annuity from an insurance company, which will give him an assured income, no matter how incorrectly he prejudges the course of security prices. Moreover, a resourceful business man, conscious of the fact that all enterprise entails a degree of speculative risk, will keep an ace in the hole in the form of an accumulation of bonds, which represent an asset wholly apart from the resources of his business. To serve its purposes, such a group of holdings should consist of high grade securities, selected with a primary emphasis on security of principal, rather than high returns or possibilities of appreciation. Moreover, to meet the varying needs of the business man, such securities should not only be of a high grade but should possess instant marketability, since in time of stress in his own business he may need quickly to convert his personal reserves into cash.

It takes a human being of some imagination and economic intelligence to forego immediate gratifications for the expectation of future realizations of happiness. And yet the economically astute will feel to a large extent repaid for avoiding the temptation to spend by the consciousness that to-morrow has to some extent been provided for. Instead of the fun of spending all surplus funds on the theater, on expensive furs, and on other vehicles of self-indulgence, the saver will have bought immunity from the worries and vague fears of poverty.

It has been wisely observed that thrift involves a transfer of part of income to capital.

Thrift also entails tying the future to the present.

CHAPTER IV

OUTLETS FOR SURPLUS FUNDS

The field of investments: stocks, bonds and tangible property.

An art, indeed, is the proper investment of money in securities. The country doctor can cover his rounds in a big, high-powered touring car that costs him two or three times what it ought to run, and the successful business man can invest his surplus in 3 per cent government bonds at par, but in both cases there is a really shocking degree of waste. Scientific management in investment, like scientific management in anything else, aims to eliminate waste. What are my needs and what is the maximum amount of income I can get out of securities filling those needs?— that is the problem with which everyone having surplus funds is faced and which only a knowledge of the principles of investment can solve.—FRANKLIN ESCHER.

ADVERTISING writers are the town criers of the present day and in an infinite variety of subtle ways they are all shrieking loudly to attract the attention of the individual. The ordinary man's total income is limited. Through advertising, the butcher, the banker, the clothier, the automobile vender and the travel bureau—to mention only a few—have enlisted all the aids that psychological research and a study of human frailties have revealed to get him to favor their offerings.

The voice of prudence and thrift is almost inaudible in the clatter of a thousand merchants boosting their wares. Only the strong willed can resist the collective pressure and retain a portion of his available funds for the quiet satisfactions to be attained through the years from intelligent investment.

What can a man do with his surplus funds?

Broadly speaking, he can acquire only one of two things. He can either buy property or wealth itself, or claims against property or wealth in the form of securities or mortgages, including insurance and savings banks deposits, both of which are secured by diversified holdings of high grade bonds.

The most common form of property purchased for investment purposes is *real estate*. Land or land buildings constitute something tangible, definite, certain. The buyer of real estate perceives precisely what he is getting. If he buys it outright—an unusual plan—no one can take it away from him or foreclose on him. It is secure within his grasp as long as society recognizes the rights of private property which confer ownership of a specified piece of

[25]

wealth on an individual, in whom title lies. The present theory which actuates society in a country like the United States is that it is socially beneficial to permit individual ownership of various forms of wealth.

Of course fortunes are made and lost in real estate. Those who pay an unduly high price for land and buildings find themselves unable to resell except at a loss. Neighborhoods change and alter values. In a steadily developing country like the United States, the perpetual growth of the population tends to add an unearned increment to the value of all well-selected real estate.

An equally common form of investment, under the present scheme of things, is the acquisition of *claims to property*. For example, A buys a house and lot for $100,000. Having only $40,000 he borrows the remaining $60,000 from B, who takes in return a first mortgage which constitutes a direct lien on the property which B has the right to take over as his own, provided A neglects to pay interest regularly and to return the principal promptly when it falls due.

The *mortgage* is a claim on the property. If a mortgage were larger and it were held by a group of individuals instead of one mortgage holder, bonds in denominations of $1,000 each might be issued with the mortgage behind them as security. These real estate first mortgage bonds, now a common form of investment, constitute claims against the property and except in form are the same as the original mortgage, of which they represent slices.

In the realm of securities, there are two broad classes—*stocks* and *bonds*.

Bonds ordinarily represent a promise of a corporation or a government to pay back a specific sum borrowed, at a specified date and in the meantime to pay a stated rate of interest. The bond holder is always a creditor of the borrower. He relies on the promise to pay of the debtor corporation or government. If the borrower fails in any essential to live up to its promises, the creditor can at once protect himself by throwing the corporation into receivership. In the case of a government, the bond holder, however, must rely upon its good faith. If a borrower fails to pay interest on bonds, its lapse is known as a default, which constitutes a black mark against its reputation and may injure its credit irreparably.

Shares of stock, on the other hand, represent part ownership in a business enterprise. The stock holder is never a creditor, but always virtually a partner. The stock holder consciously and knowingly is supposed to assume the risks of enterprise. The corporation issuing stock serves notice that it does not obligate itself in any way to pay dividends, the declaration and discontinuance of which remain matters entirely within the discretion of the board of directors whom the stockholders themselves choose to supervise the management.

There are two main classes of stocks—*common and preferred*. The dividend rate on preferred shares is usually fixed at definite rates such as 5, 6, 7, or 8 per cent.[1]

Directors must declare the full rate on the preferred stock before making any distribution on the common shares. However, except for priority over the common stock in respect to the payment of dividends and distribution of the assets of the corporation in case of liquidation, preferred shares are really junior securities on which nothing need be paid except at the will of the directors. They are subject to the prior claims as to assets and current distributions of all types of bonds of the corporation which may be outstanding.

Nothing is available for dividends on the common stock until interest on all the bonds of the corporation has been paid and until all dividend requirements on the preferred stock have been met. After all the

---

[1] For a statement of the various kinds of preferred stocks see Chap. X, "Investing without Red Tape."

prior charges have been taken care of, the residue of earnings is available for the common stock. The directors have the option of paying out all or part of the residual earnings in the form of dividends or of holding them in the treasury of the corporation for surplus account. In case of slim earnings nothing is likely to be left for the common share holders to compensate them for the use of their funds. However, in instances of an unusual success with extraordinarily large earnings, the common share holders are the chief beneficiaries, for the bond holders and preferred stock holders get only their 4, 5, 6, 7 or 8 per cent, whereas the common share holders can receive amounts limited only by the earning power of the corporation.

For the individual in quest primarily of safety of principal and assured regularity of income, common shares are the least attractive of any of the securities of a given corporation. On the other hand, for the speculator who knowingly accepts larger risks in the hope of huge profits, common shares are the most attractive of all types of securities as a vehicle for attaining his hopes.

Though the bonds of a particular corporation are always safer than the stocks of the same enterprise, it by no means follows that all bonds are more secure than all stocks. As a matter of fact, the common

[29]

stock of a well established and successful enterprise often constitutes a better investment than an underlying first mortgage bond on an experimental, poorly managed industrial concern.

The form of the security is less important than the nature of the business behind it, whether it is successful and whether its management is such as to indicate a continuance of good earnings, whether the enterprise is one of the leaders in its own line, and whether the activity of the concern is essential and reasonably permanent.

From the standpoint of form there are more varieties of bonds than of stocks.

1. *The first mortgage bond,* the oldest form of security, entails the claim against property which must be respected before all others. In case of trouble, its rights must be satisfied first. It is the safest security of the corporation which issues it. Sometimes, however, railroads use the term first mortgage in expressions like first and refunding mortgages, representing a senior lien on only a small and unimportant part of the line. It is important to look behind the name to the security itself, to ascertain whether it is really the underlying obligation.

2. The holder of a *second mortgage bond* (or subsequent mortgage such as third or fourth) occupies a midway position between the owner of prior liens,

on the one hand, and the stock holders of the borrowing corporation, on the other. His request for a return of the principal cannot be met until the claims of the first mortgage bonds have been paid in full, but he is entitled to receive the stipulated rate of interest on his bonds regardless of the fluctuating fortunes of the company. The second or junior mortgage is ordinarily created to raise more funds than it is considered safe to advance on the higher types of security, the first mortgage—and in compensation for his additional risk, the second mortgage bond holder ordinarily receives a higher rate of interest.

3. *The general mortgage bond* has been employed mainly by railroads and, to some extent, by public utility corporations to raise additional funds after the first mortgages have been placed. Usually it constitutes a first claim either upon a certain part of the company's first assets or upon lease holds or upon securities and also a second, third, fourth or later lien on other assets of the borrowing corporation.

4. *The consolidated mortgage* resembles the general mortgage except that it ordinarily does not cover the entire property of the company, but only specified assets definitely pledged. It is frequently a claim less well secured than that of the general mortgage which may already be in existence.

5. *A debenture bond* is virtually a promissory note

of the borrower. It is secured by no pledge or specific assets, but is backed by the general faith and credit of the borrower. If, however, interest is not regularly paid, the debenture bond holder like any other creditor may apply for the appointment of a receiver and force the satisfaction of his claims.

6. *An income or adjustment bond* resembles a preferred stock more than a bond. However, the directors must pay the interest on an income bond if it is actually earned, whereas in the case of preferred stock, the payment of dividends is entirely a matter of discretion. If not earned, the interest on the income bond need not be paid and the bond holders have no recourse. Usually there is a provision that back interest on income bonds must be made up before any subsequent distribution can be made in the form of dividends on stock.

7. *A collateral trust bond* resembles an ordinary bank loan which is secured by the deposit of stocks, bonds, or other negotiable paper. The bank loan usually runs only from thirty days to nine months, whereas the collateral trust bond is ordinarily designed for a more or less permanent need and may run for a score of years or more. In case of default of the collateral trust bond, the collateral goes to the bond holders who may either sell it or distribute it among themselves. The collateral trust bond is fre-

quently used as a means of financing the acquisition of securities of subsidiary corporations.

8. *A convertible bond* represents an effort to combine the elements of safety of a bond with the opportunities of speculative profits of common stock. The bond agreement of such a security ordinarily provides that at any time, or after a certain date or up to a specific time, the holder may change his bond for a fixed number of shares of stock.

9. *Equipment trust certificates* are secured by the pledge of specific equipment such as cars or locomotives, title to which is held by a trustee for the benefit of the security holders until the borrower has repaid the security holders. This form is used primarily by railroads and the borrower agrees with the trustee to pay a rental on the equipment sufficient to retire a block of the securities each year. In practice, equipment trust securities have proved singularly secure.

10. *Redeemable bonds,* which may also either be first mortgage bonds or general mortgage bonds or debentures, are those which may be retired by the borrower before the date of ultimate maturity. In other words, the borrower has the option of paying off the loan under specified conditions as to price and time before the final date when it obligates itself unconditionally to retire the bonds. Sometimes a bor-

rower sets aside special funds each year into a sinking fund for the purpose of buying up outstanding
bonds in the market and canceling them.   Another
device for achieving a similar end is through calling
in outstanding bonds for redemption, paying them off
through funds obtained through a new loan arranged
on more favorable terms.

11. *Short term notes* represent securities which ordinarily run for five years or less.   Because of the
shortness of their lifetime they are ordinarily un-
secured by a mortgage, although borrowers of inferior credit standing find it necessary to pledge securities or other negotiable collateral to secure short
term notes.

12. *Perpetual bonds* are virtually unknown in this
country, although a number of railroads have issued
bonds which mature in the twenty-first century and
which therefore, from the standpoint of the present
generation, resemble perpetual bonds.   The governments of France and Great Britian both have perpetual bonds outstanding.   British consols and French
rentes bear no promise to return the principal.   In
fact, the French security refers to no principal sum
at all, but merely reveals that the government contracts to pay the holder a fixed income—une rente—
each year.   For the permanent investor, investment
is really buying income and perpetual bonds or ob-

ligations maturing in the twenty-first century, such as issues of the Lehigh Valley, The New York Central, Louisville and Nashville, Northern Pacific, and West Shore Railroad, obviate the necessity of re-investing.

13. *Special revenue bonds* are rarely used by American borrowers, but are more frequently issued by foreign governments of inferior credit standing. Certain South American, European and Asiatic countries have pledged revenues from the sale of coffee, tobacco, and salt as security for bonds. Such revenues are definitely set aside and deposited in a bank for the benefit of the security holders or turned over to a representative of the bond holders who is stationed in the borrowing country to make sure that the contract is carried out. Ordinarily, such an arrangement is made to bolster up the credit of weak governments. However, certain American municipalities and states have issued bonds payable from a special tax. The State of North Carolina, for example, has a bond issue, the interest of which is payable from a tax on gasoline.

14. *External bonds* are those issued by a government or corporation in a foreign currency for sale to alien investors.

15. *An internal bond* is an obligation issued by a government or a corporation in terms of the currency of its own country for sale at home.

[35]

16. *A gold bond* is an obligation whose principal and interest are payable in gold coin. In the United States, this distinction has little practical meaning, for under the Gold Standard Act of 1900 the holder of any claim due in United States currency can legally demand payment in gold. In Germany, however, bonds specifically payable in gold did not depreciate with the mark, whereas other bonds were payable in virtually worthless currency.

17. *A receiver's certificate* is ordinarily a well secured obligation which is issued with permission of the court to provide for temporary needs of bankrupts and which takes precedence over all outstanding obligations of a bankrupt public utility corporation with the exception of wages and federal taxes. In some instances however, the court holds first mortgage bonds prior to the certificates. Receiver's certificates are usually short term obligations.

18. *Guaranteed bonds* are issues bearing an expressed guarantee that either principal or interest or both must be paid by the guarantor in the event of a default on the part of the borrower. Guaranteed bonds come into being frequently when a large corporation absorbs a smaller one and assumes its obligations. Examples of the best types of guaranteed bonds are the obligations of the Canadian National Railways which are guaranteed as to principal and

interest by the government of the Dominion of Canada, which owns all the capital stock of the railroad system.

19. *Assumed bonds* are those in which the obligation for payment has been taken over by another company which has bought or leased the property of the issuing company. They differ from the guaranteed bond in that they bear no notice on their face of the assumption of such liability.

20. *Tax exempt bonds* are those which are free from federal or state impost. Obligations of states and municipalities are exempt from federal taxes and from state taxes in the state in which they were issued. Income from prewar securities of the United States Government and the first Liberty 3½s and Federal Land Bank and joint stock land bank bonds are fully tax exempt. Income on other Liberty Bonds and from War Savings Certificates is exempt from the normal income tax when the amount of such securities does not exceed specified sums. Income from corporate bonds is subject to full federal taxes unless the borrower has agreed to pay all or part of the tax due. Many corporations have undertaken to pay the normal income tax on their obligations up to two per cent.

CHAPTER V

THE MIND OF THE SMALL INVESTOR

Financial aims and purposes of individuals of limited means.

There has been a significant increase in the purchases and sales of small lots of stock, and a corresponding decrease in the transfers of large blocks. Whatever the fundamental causes of this tendency, it has had the effect of extending the facilities of the Stock Exchange to thousands of new and small investors all over the country, whose frequent inexperience with security investment has placed and is placing an increased moral responsibility upon the Exchange itself, as well as causing changes and improvements in many parts of its system.—SEYMOUR L. CROMWELL.

PRIOR to 1914, there were not more than 400,000 bond holders in the United States, and the great masses of men used to look upon bond holders as "bloated." This conception changed when many millions of plain men and women acquired Liberty bonds for patriotic reasons during the war. A prompt but silent revolution took place when multitudes who became bond holders touched for the first time an engraved cer-

[38]

tificate of indebtedness and became coupon clippers.

The educational value of the Liberty loan campaigns has not been entirely lost. The impulse to invest survived, but has been frequently misdirected by unscrupulous stock venders to the extent of more than $500,000,000 a year for the last five years.

No generalization about the mental processes of the new investor will hold true universally, unless it applies to all human beings, for the new investing classes are composed of all kinds of men and women.

Many small investors are in quest of securities giving the highest yield "consistent with safety." They pay at least lip service to the element of security, but there is something contradictory in their aim. Economists know that, other things being equal, as the yield or income on a bond increases, the factor of safety tends to decline. A bond yielding more than taxable United States Government obligations, which sell at a price consonant with the true interest rate or rental value of money, entails larger risks and the excess yield represents insurance against greater hazards.

The small investor frequently inquires whether a particular stock represents a safe speculation. His is a fantastic quest, something like a search for dry water, or still motion, for, if a proposition is safe, its securities would be investment issues, assuring safety of principal and regularity of income. Speculative securities are necessarily more or less unsafe, and the principal motive of speculators is to attain an appreciation of principal and income in return for the greater risks assumed.

Moreover, the uninitiated investor frequently has a private suspicion that the banker or financial editor or other adviser has up his sleeve some perfectly safe and highly profitable proposition which out of perversity he will not pass on except to friends. The truth is that no one is exempt from possible loss from speculative securities.

Out of a great mass of letters received from small investors came a clear demonstration of the fact that *the person with a definite thrift program gets further along the road to financial independence than the aimless ones.*

Accumulation of wealth is to a degree independent of the precise income of the investor. Many thriftless men with an income of $25,000 a year have difficulty in living within their means, whereas others, averaging no more than $2,000 a year, regularly and persistently throughout the years allocate a part of their income to their savings accounts.

What counts in the financial set-up is not how much a man's gross earnings are, but his net income at the end of the year; the difference between what comes in

[40]

The Mind of the Small Investor

and what goes out. Financial intelligence does not fluctuate in accordance with the size of one's pocketbook.

The records show, moreover, that the new capitalist, who for the first time has been accumulating bonds and high grade stocks, has not developed independence at the expense of the savings banks and life insurance companies.

One adverse tendency on the part of the small buyer is to make inquiries about promotion stocks *after* he has purchased them instead of *before*.

The small investor should learn to keep in as close touch with developments affecting his holdings as the large security owner if he would avoid loss. He should clip coupons when they fall due for if he leaves them uncashed he not only loses interest on the sum involved, but in exceptional cases the coupon itself may become valueless. The Norwegian government, for example, has passed a law that drawn bonds not presented for payment within twenty years and coupons not cashed within ten years after due date become void.

On called bonds the loss of interest after the redemption date may be very large. Investors should scan the financial pages of the newspapers for information as to offers of exchange of securities and rights to subscribe to new issues.

Common Sense of Money and Investments

The amateur investor sometimes blunders unbelievably in attending to the routine matters in protection of his holdings. The failure to exercise valuable rights, delay in clipping coupons, tardiness in presenting for payment bonds which have been called for redemption, and general carelessness cost investors in the aggregate a colossal sum each year, wholly apart from money lost through swindlers and bad judgment in the selection of securities. By way of illustration, the courts recently ordered the divorce of the coal properties from the railroad properties of the Lehigh Valley Railroad Company. For a dollar a share stockholders had the right to acquire the coal stock which was worth about $35 a share. The right to subscribe expired on June 15, 1924, and 18,273 rights were unused. Through carelessness, ignorance or inattention shareholders sacrificed valuable privileges of high market worth. The court, however, stepped in on behalf of the financially illiterate and extended the period until the following October 15th. The experience of the United States Treasury Department reveals similar traits.

Owners of Liberty bonds are, in many instances, failing to collect what is rightfully theirs.

In connection with all the Liberty bond issues (except the first 3½s) coupon bonds were originally issued with only a partial array of interest coupons

[42]

attached and were later exchangeable for permanent coupon bonds with all the interest coupons to maturity attached. On April 30, 1924, 399,039 Liberty bond pieces had not yet been exchanged and as a result $4,767,979 of past due interest had not been collected.

Moreover, there was outstanding on the same date, a total of $22,552,480 of matured debt on which interest had ceased. Included in this amount was $156,100 of Victory 3¾s, which were called for redemption on June 15, 1922; $5,660,350 of Victory 4¾s with serial letters A to F which were called on December 15, 1922, and $10,331,950 of Victory 4¾s with serial letters from G to S which matured on May 20, 1923. There remained outstanding on the same date War Savings Certificates of the series of 1918, which matured on January 1, 1923, in amount of $13,790,915; and War Savings Certificates of the series of 1919 which matured on January 1, 1924, in amount of $7,707,050 maturity value. Moreover, matured interest obligations, representing past due interest checks and interest coupons which had not been presented for payment were outstanding on the same date in total amount $67,-611,240.

Furthermore, the 4 per cent bonds of the first Liberty loan have been convertible into 4¼ per cent bonds since June 15, 1919, and the same privilege has been given to the bonds of the second Liberty Loan since May 15, 1919. Many holders of the 4 per cent bonds have failed to take advantage of the exchange which would have added ¼ per cent to their income. On April 30 there remained outstanding 43,298 pieces of the first 4s, with a par value of $7,426,100, and 174 pieces of the second 4s with a par value of $30,043,650.

Each security holder should look over his own list and ascertain whether any exchanges are necessary. When in doubt he should write directly to an officer of the company whose securities he owns. Those who are compelled to travel, or who for any reason are unable to supervise their own holdings, can get a bank or trust company to act as financial secretary at a nominal charge. The careful investor will make periodic examination of his holdings at least once or twice a year to check up on their current investment merit and on possible exchanges or redemptions.

CHAPTER VI

THE RADICAL AND HIS BONDS

Political theories versus financial expediencies.

Modern Socialism has no designs upon the money in a man's pocket. It is quite true that the earlier and extreme Socialist theorists did in their communism find no use for money, but I do not think there are any representative Socialists now who do not agree that the state must pay and receive in money, that *money is indispensable to human freedom.* The featurelessness of money, its universal convertability, gives human beings a latitude of choice and self-expression in its spending that is inconceivable without its use.—H. G. WELLS.

SELF interest—the underlying motive of the present economic scheme of things—makes strange bedfellows. It sometimes causes Socialists to finance capitalism and capitalists to provide the financial sinews for state Socialism.

Since high wartime and post-war super taxes have come to plague our multimillionaires the investment habits of the very rich have been significantly altered. The excessively well-to-do have found an escape from the pain of turning over nearly half their income from investments to the government in tax exempt securities such as the first Liberty 3½s and the obligations of the various states and municipalities of the United States. In putting the major portion of their funds in local and national government securities, these arch capitalists—the great believers in the rights of private property—have been pouring their funds without reservation into furthering activities that come broadly under the head of state Socialism.

To men of middle grade incomes, the tax exemption feature in securities has been less alluring. In this group are not a few parlor Socialists and radicals. They buy leisure for themselves in the form of securities of private corporations which they loathe. They get time to preach anti-capitalism partly as a result of their income from funds invested in capitalistic enterprises.

Occasionally one meets professionally anti-capitalist politicians and lay citizens. If they happen to own B. M. T. stocks or bonds, however, they make a separate pigeonhole in their minds for this corporation and exempt it from their wrath and fury. When matters arise affecting the worth of their own holdings they are inclined to insist on full protection of their constitutional guarantees in the courts.

[46]

The Radical and His Bonds

The effect on security prices would be very great if the rantings and ravings of the apostles of discontent were quickly translated into action. Yet many of the emotional economists are themselves security owners and in the later rôle would object strenuously to any activities that impair the obligation of contract.

It is perhaps well that citizens do not vote and talk politics exclusively in accordance with the importunities of their own pocketbooks.

Any large or small investor ought to be willing to sacrifice his own holdings as the price for the attaining of Don Marquis's "Almost Perfect State."

On the other hand, it is seemingly feasible for an individual to remain in good standing in the radical and socialist movement and at the same time build up a well conceived investment structure.

Morris Hillquit, a leader of Socialism in America, has prepared for this chapter an expression of the Socialist attitude toward financing capitalism.

"Individual investments and choice of securities, in my opinion," Mr. Hillquit explained, "present exactly the same question to Socialists and Radicals as they do to individualists and reactionaries. The Socialist is opposed to the economic system which permits of unearned revenues in the shape of rent, interest and profits. He seeks to substitute that system

[47]

by one based on the principle of coöperative labor
and equitable distribution of the product. He expects that system to be brought about by a series of
economic and legal reforms on a national, even international scale and not through individual practices. The economic system operates equally on all
persons, regardless of the political or social views
held by them. A Socialist or Radical cannot by his
own individual act withdraw himself from the operation of the system while it lasts. He can find place
only in the established economic categories as employer, worker, professional, etc. If he earns or
otherwise acquires money, he can put it only to such
uses as the system affords to him. He would ac-
complish no good by throwing it away or keeping it
in a strong box. If he has any money to invest, he
must look for safe and profitable investment in the
ordinary way.

"Purely as a matter of sentiment, a Socialist or
Radical would, in my opinion, ordinarily discriminate against securities of particularly odious concerns such, for instance, as are largely based upon the
exploitation of child labor, pursuit in notorious anti-
union policy, etc."

CHAPTER VII

TESTS OF A SAFE INVESTMENT

Footrules by which the worth of a security may be measured.

Judging the value of a bond is no different from judging the value of a house or a horse or anything else—it is simply a question of knowing the principles which apply. One horse is built for speed, another for dragging heavy loads, yet the same general principles enable the experienced dealer to tell the value of either almost at a glance. So it is with bonds.—FRANKLIN ESCHER.

THE steel engraver plays no favorites.

He produces certificates of strong and emaciated financial institutions with equal care. The soundest bond and the most fanciful stock resemble each other in physical texture.

Neither weighing nor feeling will aid the investment amateur in discriminating among certificates. Worthless securities which paper the walls of many a disillusioned hopeful, are invariably neatly engraved, and reflect dignity and trustworthiness.

The sense of touch helps the buyer to select textiles.

The sense of smell aids in choosing beverages.

The sense of sight protects the purchaser of works of art.

The sense of hearing guides the buyer of musical instruments.

The sense of taste charts the course of the consumer of food.

But the animal from which man has evolved has no simple intuitive means of separating the wheat from the chaff in securities.

Stocks and bonds constitute no natural product of the soil. They are inventions of the human mind, and are the outgrowth of a highly complex economic civilization. Instinct is an unsafe guide in this new realm, in which intelligence controls.

Securities are not things, but symbols.

Behind good stocks and bonds is an infinite variety of commodities and tools, which man has fashioned out of elemental clay. Great factories, industrial laboratories, market-places, steel rails, massive terminals, and vast accumulations of the infinite commodities of barter are the realities back of the steel engraved certificates of prosperous, going concerns.

Behind seemingly identical certificates of prospects and blue sky promotions are merely hot air, hopes and fanciful aspirations.

[50]

Tests of a Safe Investment

In order to discriminate, the security buyer theoretically ought, if possible, himself or through the eyes of an expert to examine the plants, machinery, inventory and other claimed assets which impart value and earning power to the corporations whose stocks or bonds he is urged to buy. Sometimes, these corporate possessions will be scattered widely across the full expanse of the continent, and it is obviously impracticable for the buyer of a single share of $100 par value stock to undertake so comprehensive an investigation.

Modern finance, however, consists of more than you can see and touch. The mortar which holds together the colossal industrial structure of the present generation is faith. Credit, which consists of confidence in other men, is the dynamic force which motivates economic life. The crucial choice then comes in deciding whom to trust. That decision, made many times each day, is the principal job, by the way, of the banker, who picks out the business men in whom he believes and then through granting credit guarantees their solvency up to the extent of their line of credit to the whole commercial world.

Certified public accountants are the agents of society who under definite legal and ethical restrictions undertake to examine the actual assets and liabilities of a corporation, and certify to their authenticity for the benefits of creditors and security holders. Thus the investor who of course cannot visit the oil fields of the Mid-continent district, or hydro-electric plants in California, or a road of iron stretching from Chicago to Omaha can get a reliable check on the assertions of the sponsors of the corporation from the report of expert bookkeepers.

A financial statement, of course, is like an editorial in a newspaper—a statement of opinion. But, if the accountants are neither dupes nor crooks, it will tend to be an accurate expression. The balance sheet gives a cross section picture of the corporation at a particular moment in its history, usually on December 31, sometimes on June 30, or in other cases whenever its fiscal year happens to end. Since all is relative, the meaning of the figures in a balance sheet will become pregnant with significance only if compared with similar reports of earlier years. The moving tale of what has occurred in the twelvemonth between the periodical photographing of assets and liabilities is ordinarily termed the income account, which reveals whether the management has succeeded in amassing profits.

Figures frequently lie, but never permit a vender of securities to refuse to produce financial statements on the ground that they are misleading anyway. The production of a fake balance sheet or

[52]

income account constitutes a serious criminal offense, and the charlatan ordinarily will prefer not to assume the risk. On the other hand, there are subtle ways in which a corporation's reports may understate or exaggerate the worth of its assets, and yet keep within the law.

A safe investment is one which involves a high degree of security of principal and assured regularity of income. The highest security is ordinarily found primarily in the best grade of bonds and mortgages, which are evidences of indebtedness, representing a contract to return the principal sum at a specified date and meantime to pay interest at a fixed rate. Shares, common and preferred, particularly the latter, frequently possess investment characteristics, which give them a suitable place in the holdings even of individuals who are not concerned mainly with the speculative aim of appreciation of principal.

Absolute safety is theoretically unattainable. Approximate safety is the best that human beings can search for in this fluid world of earthquakes, revolutions, and catastrophes. Bonds of the highest grade possess all reasonable assurances of continued safety, and that is all any one has the right to expect.

Under existing circumstances, obligations of the United States Treasury represent par in the scheme of investment things. The debt of the government, though large, is well within the limit of the nation's resources and wealth creating capacity. Hence there is no question of *ability to pay*—the first test of a government's credit. The next criterion is *willingness to pay*, which is concerned with good faith. Public opinion, backed by constitutional and statutory law, in the United States, seems overwhelmingly in favor of keeping the faith in financial transactions.

As Andrew W. Mellon recently pointed out, "The good faith of the American people to meet their public obligations finds full expression in our tax system. Regardless of honest differences of opinion as to what constitutes the best and most equitable system of taxation, public sentiment in the United States is unanimous in approving taxes sufficiently high to pay the legitimate running expenses of the government and to effect the gradual reduction of the public debt."

All this seems obvious enough. But defaults on foreign government obligations have not been infrequent. The largest defaulter to-day is Russia, and the failure of that country to meet its obligations currently is ascribable to the lack of the will rather than of the ability to pay. At this writing Mexico, after a decade in default, not because of inability, is just returning to good financial society, having agreed to try to resume debt service. Sometimes a nation falls down, not through lack of will, but through sheer lack of capacity. Germany's reparation obligations are in a somewhat different category, but her default has been ascribed by competent independent economists to the fact that the terms fixed in the London agreement of 1921 exceeded the capacity of the Reich to pay.

A clue to the intentions of various peoples may be found in their history, which is readily accessible in such a convenient handbook as *Kimber's Record of Government Debts and Foreign Securities.*

Evolution concerns ethics as well as physical characteristics, and it would be misleading to assume that a nation which once slipped from the graces should be eternally damned in the world's money capitals. Previous falls from a plane of rectitude, however, are factors which determine the credit of a would-be borrower, and the rate of interest required.

The first test of a government's credit is its good faith, for nations, unlike individual debtors, are sovereign bodies which cannot be haled into court.

In this country, the idea of using human lives and bayonets to validate contracts between foreign governments and native investors does not thrill the democracy. The investor in alien government bonds should be conscious of the fact that he is assuming the risk of non-payment, and should not expect the Federal Government to employ the Navy and Marine Corps when necessary to correct his mistakes of judgment, although Great Britain has frequently seen fit to do so. Various factors in recent years have operated to heighten the sense of financial honor in Latin America, whereas the extravagance of the Great War has tended to weaken the credit of the principal European nations, whose indebtedness climbed so prodigously as to impair their ability to pay. In the past, the sense of honor in connection with meeting national indebtedness was, in general, higher in Europe than in South America. In the Old World, the small island of England came to dominate half the universe in a financial sense because of its long standing punctiliousness in meeting obligations promptly as they fall due.

A country's ability to pay is measured by the extent of its resources and of its annual social income. Debt charges which exceed the difference between the necessary costs of running a government and the amount of the total social income which may safely be taken in the form of taxation signalize precarious financing, which, unless the situation is corrected, foreshadows defaults or the scaling down of debts. A nation, which does not keep its total expenditures, including debt charges, within its receipts from revenues, is pursuing a course which leads to ruin, although for temporary emergencies, such as wars, the abnormal policy may properly be followed.

If taxes are so high as to compel nations to dip into their accumulations of capital, a nation is moving into hazardous ground.

A nation which finances itself through endless borrowing either from investors or from central banks, causing inflation, is proceeding unsoundly.

Weaker governments will sometimes seek to heighten the value of their bonds by making them constitute liens on certain public properties, such as the salt or tobacco monopoly. These mortgages are of little value unless supported by the good faith of the borrowing government. Liens on customs receipts, where agents of the lender collect the customs, are better assurances of payment, though submission to such an arrangement is usually distasteful to a free and independent government. Countries of weak credit, such as Jugo-Slavia, San Salvador, Brazil and China have had to resort to this course.

Corporation bonds spring from a different set of circumstances.

Willingness to pay fades into insignificance, because the courts are ready to enforce contracts. Capacity to pay becomes of paramount importance. The bankruptcy courts are perpetually replete with men of excellent intentions who would pay if they could. Failure in business results infinitely more frequently from incompetence than from malevolence.

American railroads have been good and bad to investors who supported them.

Most of the larger systems have been through reorganizations, a polite term for a process of notifying the stock and junior bondholders that their holdings have been either wiped out or scaled down for the benefit of the property, its senior bondholders, and the public.

Underlying closed first mortgage bonds on the larger American railroads, however, have stood the test of fire, and have come through receiverships and readjustments unimpaired. Even a first mortgage on a weak system which runs through a district which needs steam transportation service is ordinarily suitable for investment purposes. In fact, some experts prefer first mortgages on essential, but weak, systems to second, third, and fourth mortgages on strong lines. Usually both classes of railroad bonds are available at about the same price.

Junior bonds of a prosperous company bear a premium, which capitalizes superior management, which some argue may be supplanted by less efficient officers and directors before the bond matures. Underlying first mortgages on weaker roads, however,

[58]

have seemingly discounted in their low prices, in relation to quotations on first mortgages of strong systems, inferiority of management or capital structure. The worst is already known, and there may be improvement before the bond is paid off. That is how some investment bankers argue, yet others prefer junior liens of successes, emphasizing that earning power is the necessary attribute of a business concern.

Under the Transportation Act of 1920, Congress has for the first time interested itself in assuring a fair return on the actual property value of the railroads. But the legislative body has merely signified good intentions; it has guaranteed nothing. The Interstate Commerce Commission, under the constructions in the Act, fixes rates so that large regional groups shall earn a fair return, at present defined as $5\frac{3}{4}$ per cent. But since within regional groups there are various types of efficiency of management, some systems earn more than the fair return and some less. To keep the efficient from profiteering, the Act provides that one half of the excess over 6 per cent should be transferred to the national treasury.

The effect of the Act has been to stabilize and improve railroad earning power, and to validate bonds of soundly financed railroad corporations. The

[59]

measure of earning power is gross income, and the margin of safety over interest and dividend requirements are shown in net earnings, which are reported monthly under uniform conditions laid down by the Interstate Commerce Commission. Under the present scheme of railroad regulation, the railroads have fewer secrets and mysteries than industrial corporations, which often conceal the story of success or failure from the vast republic of security holders for at least twelve months until the publication of the annual report, which is of course ancient history from a speculative standpoint.

As the small investor comes to exercise his new and growing influence, the tendency will be to force all corporations whose securities are widely distributed to publish monthly reports of earnings and expenses. Some of the larger industrial corporations, such as the United States Steel Corporation, which is a model for the fullness and amplitude of its financial publicity, issues quarterly reports of earnings. Where a company remains silent except once a year, it gives a tremendous potential advantage to officers, directors, and their friends, who, if lacking in a high sense of ethics, might exploit the relative ignorance of other security holders. Fairness entails placing all investors on an equality with respect to promptness of information concerning the welfare of the property, unless it can be demonstrated beyond a shadow of doubt that publicity will give an advantage to competitors.

Public utility concerns, like the railways, are under close state supervision, and are generally required to publish reliable monthly reports.

The value of a public utility security is conditioned somewhat by the political attitude of the community. Having recognized this fact recently, the utility corporations have embarked on a significant career of multiplying their friends through inviting their customers to become partners by buying a few shares of stock.[1]

Earning power is determined by agreement with the public authorities as to a proper return on the investment. The permanent desirability of long term utility bonds is affected by the nature of the franchise, particularly as to whether it is unrevocable. An appeal to the courts against so-called confiscatory rates has latterly provided a new basis of safety for utility investors. The doctrine that such enterprises are entitled to a fair return on their property has been enunciated.

A traction company, a power and light, or a telephone company in a growing community of diversified industries seems better safeguarded against the

---

[1] See Chap. XXV, "The Customer Buys the Plant."

[61]

exigencies of the future than a company in a receding city, wholly dependent on one large industry, such as silk mills, which are subject to the ebb and flow of public demand for that particular product.

The margin of safety over interest and dividend requirements through the various phases of the business cycle indicates the soundness of a security. Ordinarily, a public utility will earn a smaller margin over such requirements in years of prosperity than an industrial enterprise, but the slump in adverse years will likewise be less marked. Restrictions as to the issuance of new securities should be carefully studied from two standpoints: first, are the holders of outstanding securities protected against discrimination in favor of new issues; and secondly, is the company retaining sufficient freedom to finance its future growth.

Stable prices are helpful to utility corporations, which suffered drastically during and after the war from rising commodity prices. The utility companies were unable to get their rates increased as fast as prices climbed. Thus their surpluses were in many cases effaced; dividends were stopped; and the payment of interest on bonds became difficult. When prices began to decline, the effects were diametrically opposite, for the public utility rates were slower to come down.

Tests of a Safe Investment

The companies which fared worst and are in general least desirable from an investment standpoint are those which contracted with municipal authorities to furnish service at a fixed rate, irrespective of any changes in the purchasing power of money.

Unlike railroads and public utilities, industrial corporations are free agents in business. They can do as they please, provided they do not violate the law. In many states, they are required to issue no reports and are subject to no supervision unless, brought into the courts for a specific offense.

In general, this quality of liberty makes industrial corporations more attractive to shareholders than to bondholders, for there is always the hope, usually futile, of fabulous earnings. If the return on capital is more than the ordinary interest rate, the shareholders, who get the residue, are the sole direct beneficiaries. Moreover, the earnings of most industrial corporations fluctuate dramatically from periods of prosperity to eras of adversity. Stability, rather than fits and starts, is desired by bondholders, whose first aim is security.

Long term industrial bonds deserve consideration only when secured by a concern whose product is essential and likely to remain so through the years. Securities of companies producing passing fads and fancies are highly speculative in character and need

[63]

not interrupt the quest of the investor for stability and safety.

Buyers of industrial bonds should determine whether the company involved is a powerful factor in an essential industry, which in all probability can stand up well against all competitors, present and prospective. The question of whether it has an assured supply of raw materials, preferably under its own control, is also relevant. A concern which can stand on its own legs and sell goods because of superior quality and price is better, from an investment standpoint, than one which survives solely by virtue of a protective tariff, and which may be toppled from its pedestal of artificial prosperity by the election of a free trade party.

It is difficult to divorce the speculative element from industrial corporations. The New York State law has recognized this in failing to characterize any industrial bonds as legal investment for savings banks. Of course, general legislative tests of this character are clumsy, and sometimes unfair. Few corporation bonds of any character bear a higher degree of safety, for example, than United States Steel sinking fund 5s. Moreover, the New York law still, for less good reasons now that the position of this class of securities has improved, discriminates against public utility bonds, although a movement is under way to rescind this inhibition.

The principal test of the value of an industrial security is earning power, backed by ample assets in case of liquidation.

From the long term viewpoint, the social utility of an enterprise is an important consideration for the investor. In an intelligent society, business concerns which do not meet this test are likely eventually to fail. Since notions of utility change from generation to generation, it is not always easy to foresee future standards. Two decades ago, the ordinary individual would have been willing to tie up funds in a profitable brewery, which the subsequent prohibition laws tend to render obsolete.

Marketability in a security gives an investor an opportunity to correct his mistakes of judgment and hence is a necessary attribute.

CHAPTER VIII

WHY NOT GET RICH QUICK?

The lesson of the lotteries and gaming tables.

If I gamble I practically gamble with society whose re-
sources are unlimited, while my resources are limited.
And the limit of my resources results in my disadvantage.
If I begin with a thousand pounds, even if I gain a million
I may lose it again; but if I once reach a net loss of a
thousand I can never retrieve it, for I have nothing more to
stake. This is the basis of the disadvantage of gambling.
—W. A. WHITWORTH.

PARADOXICALLY enough, those offering so-called
get-rich-quick securities are almost invariably fakers,
whereas those with a genuine one-out-of-a-million opportunity are inclined to understate its prospects.

The genuine initiator of any project recognizes the
existence of business risk; he sees the hazards and
the danger as well as the alluring possibilities for constructive effort. The charlatan, on the other hand,
in presenting his proposition, is silent concerning
the element of risk and pretends it is non-existent.

Professional advisers to investors level their severest blow at an enterprise when they characterize
it as a get-rich-quick proposition. If the get-rich-

quick enterprise were what its name seems to imply, the appellation would really be one of fulsome praise rather than a tag of damnation. For, in spite of the preachments of the financially chaste, the ordinary mortal still secretly nourishes a hope of making a lucky strike which will suddenly transform him into a man of great wealth. But experience has shown that so-called get-rich-quick opportunities might better be characterized as lose-your-principal-ultimately securities.

Sometimes the incredulous investor is heard to remark "I wish my banker would tell me what he buys himself, instead of what he thinks is good for me." If the banker in his own investments sometimes departs from the standards of financial rectitude, he does so consciously, knowing that he is assuming larger than ordinary risks. Investment infallibility, especially as one strays from the obviously high grade issues, does not exist and financiers on the very inside of a proposition frequently misjudge its prospects and opportunities.

Frequently the lay buyer of cats and dogs—as the lowly in the security world are known—entrusts his funds knowing his prospects of success are no greater than one in a hundred, but, swept by the gambler's instincts, he prefers the unlikelihood of making a "killing" to the certainty of 5 per cent.

[67]

An individual of such tastes might better vent his passions in the lotteries and at the gaming tables. Where these gambling devices are permitted to operate in accordance with the laws of chance, he faces better prospects than as a consumer of beautifully engraved certificates reflecting nothing but the false promises of blue sky promoters.

There is of course, no economic justification for gambling. Apart from the ethics of the case, gambling is an economically wasteful activity. It is different in kind from speculation. Speculation, which is inevitable in this world of uncertainties, entails the assumption of necessary risks, such as the hazard as to whether the next wheat crop will be large or small or whether the demand for automobiles will be greater or less than in the previous season. Such economic risks exist in the nature of things and the business man or farmer can in a measure shift them to speculators whose rôle it is to assume hazards and forecast the future.

Gambling, on the other hand, entails the assumption of unnecessary risks, such as whether a tossed coin will show the head or the tail or whether one thoroughbred will trot faster on a race course than another. No one has to undertake such hazards and the gambler, unlike the speculator, is relieving no one else in assuming them.

Why not Get Rich Quick?

Investment is entirely different from gambling, but differs only in degree from speculation. Investing represents a quest for safety of principal and assured regularity of income, whereas in speculation the incentive is to attain an appreciation of principal rather than mere security.

Men otherwise intelligent, who in their financial relations become intoxicated with the hopes of excessive gain, frequently place their funds consciously in unpromising and far fetched speculations. They will buy almost anything that a plausible promoter presents because they are acting on the theory that the law of averages is certain eventually to bring them something good and that the one success will more than pay for the thousand failures. Silly reasoning! In order to be sure the law of averages would eventually lead one to the financial paradise it might be necessary to live ten thousand years. Moreover, the average worth of valueless securities is zero.

Get-rich-quick propositions are always seemingly on the bargain counter. Those promoting them perpetually send stock salesmen into the cities and into the countryside. Common sense would indicate even to the inexpert buyer that those with a proposition that assured quick riches would not need to employ security peddlers to unload stocks by high pressure methods on an unwary public.

[69]

CHAPTER IX

INVESTING WITHOUT RED TAPE

Conveniences of preferred stock.

Standard Oil preferred stock is better than most bonds. United States Steel preferred is an investment security of great strength. Still preferred stock investment is not to be made without watching the business. If things go wrong, there is little equity, as debts must be paid first. If things go poorly, the lapse of dividends is apt to be longer than expected.—MORREL W. GAINES.

PREFERRED stocks of strong companies are like common shares in form and like bonds in spirit.

Ordinarily, preferred issues are wholly unsuited for builders of financial castles in the air who expect untold riches from a small investment. Usually the return on preferred shares is definitely limited to 5, 6, 7, or 8 per cent, as the case may be. Those who dream fantastically of infinitely larger returns (with corresponding risks) must turn to common shares, where the dividends are limited only by the capacity of an enterprise to make money.

Preferred shares, like common, represent a partnership interest in a business concern, not a debt, like a bond. There is no legal obligation for directors to declare dividends on preferred shares, except that none can be paid on the common before the stipulated payments on the preferred have been made. In the case of bonds, on the other hand, where the interest rate is fixed at a definite rate, payment must be paid promptly, or the security holders can throw the company into receivership.

To a legalistically minded person it sometimes appears that preferred shareholders must assume all the risk of failure and depression, without the compensating feature of unlimited returns, such as common shares have, in case of an overwhelming period of prosperity. In this pragmatic world, however, it frequently happens that preferred shares of well financed companies receive dividends without interruption all through the ebb and flow of the business cycle, whereas common shares, which sometimes partake of the rôle of prince and sometimes of pauper, receive only intermittent payments.

The mere names of securities, taken by themselves, are likely to be highly deceptive to the amateur. Preferred stocks of a company, such as the National Biscuit Company, are at present the senior securities, with no bonds outranking them, and are strongly safeguarded by large assets and huge earning power.

On the other hand, each day promoters are offering so-called preferred shares which capitalize merely their hopes, aspirations, and hot air. Legal distinctions in the last analysis mean little to the investor, who must tear through the maze of pretense to the reality of the corporation behind the stock—its physical properties, its character of management, and its financial history and outlook.

In the case of well established corporations, which have tangible property behind every dollar of their securities and whose preferred shares have a long dividend paying record, directors are disposed to look upon preferred shares as investment securities which have been bought primarily for relative safety of principal and assured regularity of income. On the other hand, they frequently regard their common shares as speculative, indicating that the holders are consciously assuming larger risks in the hope of extraordinary returns. Thus, when financial storms blow up, they are infinitely less reluctant to pass the common dividend than the preferred. Moreover, they will readily dip into surplus, which represents the accumulation of excess earning in the past, to keep up their preferred disbursements, whereas they would hesitate to do so in case of dividends on common stocks.

Moreover, most preferred shares are cumulative,

which means that in the case of default of dividends the back payments must be made up before any disbursement can be made on the common shares. Preferred shares have preference over the common ordinarily, not only in respect to dividends, but also in reference to assets in case of the dissolution of the company. Non-cumulative preferred shares are entitled to the preference as to dividends only at the time they are scheduled to be paid. In case of default, the back payments are forgotten.[1]

Unlike bonds, preferred shares usually involve no obligation on the part of the issuing corporation to redeem them at a stipulated date at their face value. Usually they nominally can remain outstanding forever, although frequently the company retains the privilege of redeeming them at a stipulated price, usually above par. The fact that bonds represent an obligation which must be paid off in full at the maturity date makes fluctuation in the price of high grade bonds of purely theoretical significance to the permanent investor. In the case of stocks, however, the security holder can reimburse himself, ordinarily,

[1] In the U. S. Cast Iron Pipe & Foundry case, however, the Court of Errors and Appeals in New Jersey held (Oct. 1924) that owners of non-cumulative preferred stock have a claim on a given year's dividends if earned, even though not declared, and that no common dividend may be paid until such disbursements are made to the preferred stockholders.

only through selling the issues for what they will bring at the open market place.

As compared with bonds, preferred shares of the same companies usually bear a higher rate of return to the investor. Moreover, unlike bonds and like common stocks, preferred shares are free from the normal income tax. Furthermore, whereas interest coupons on bonds must be clipped and presented for payment, dividends are sent through the mail to stockholders. As compared with common stocks, preferred are more attractive in cases of corporations of stabilized and relatively certain earning power than of concerns whose profits are a thing of great uncertainty. Unless the investor is reasonably sure of getting his dividends on preferred shares, he might better acquire the common and place himself in a position to receive large returns in a case of success. Better still, he might eschew buying the securities of a corporation whose earning power is a matter of conjecture.

Frequently the voting power of a corporation rests solely with the common stockholders. To the small investor the lack of a franchise makes little practical difference, but to large interests it is often a controlling factor in choosing between common and preferred shares. Often a provision is made that, in case of inability to pay preferred dividends for a

[74]

stated period, preferred shares gain voting power which the common shares lose.

In general, railroad and public utility corporations, whose earning power is restricted by law, lend themselves to preferred stock issues, because they have stability of earning power which preferred shareholders desire. Industrial corporations, on the other hand, with unlimited theoretical earning power, but without the stability of a regulated monopoly are more essentially speculative and make their appeal primarily to buyers of common stocks.

In buying preferred shares of an industrial promotion, the security buyer would be assuming tremendous risks without the hope of commensurate return. And yet, in the case of strongly entrenched industrial corporations with a commanding position in their field, preferred stocks such as those of the National Biscuit Company, United States Steel Corporation, American Car & Foundry Company, American Tobacco Company, and American Bank Note Company are suitable for investment purposes and are surpassed by few, if any, railroad and public utility preferred issues.

The individual investor in quest of sound securities is scarcely interested in exceptions and negations. He is less concerned with the difficulties of generalization than with the setting up of guideposts which enable him to separate the sheep from the goats in the investment world.

As a practical rule of thumb guide to good preferred stocks, the following tests are suggested;

1. *Would there be adequate tangible property behind the preferred stock, after all the bonds and other debts of the corporation were paid off?*

2. *Is the demonstrated earning power over a period of years—not the prospective or "maybe" earning power—equal to the preferred stock dividends with an ample margin to take care of fluctuations in the normal business cycle?*

3. *Is there a substantial block of dividend paying common stock junior to the preferred outstanding to assume the shocks and speculative risks of the business?*

4. *Does the company occupy a commanding or at least a superior place in its industry?*

5. *Is the company engaged in an essential and relatively stable and permanent industry?*

6. *Is the preferred issue safeguarded by priority as to assets, by at least conditional voting power, by cumulative provisions, by a power to veto proposed obligations which would have a prior claim on earnings and assets?*

7. *Is the preferred issue callable and is the redemption price above the present market value?*

[76]

CHAPTER X

INVESTMENT PROGRAMS FOR RICH AND POOR

Specific recommendations for the workingman, the business man, the lawyer, the doctor, the minister, and other classes.

If you want to know whether you are destined to be a success or failure in life, you can easily find out. The test is simple and it is infallible. Are you able to save money? If not, drop out. You will lose. You may think not, but you will lose as sure as you live. The seed of success is not in you.—JAMES J. HILL.

To the uninitiated it would appear that the investments needs of all two-legged mammals are precisely the same. Before careful analysis of the problem, one might assume that securities are either good or bad, sound or unsound, and that the bonds of a solvent corporation would be suitable for the race track man, the club woman, the scientific bridge player, the widow dependent upon the income from securities, and the prosperous man of business. However, in the investment world, what is sauce for the goose may not necessarily be sauce for the gander.

A successful business man may, let us assume, place funds in an experimental concern, which seems destined to produce no dividends for five years but which later is likely to yield profits out of the ordinary. Perhaps it is a scheme for taking the frying-pan sizzle out of radio receiving sets. Not needing the funds thus tied up in illiquid securities, he can afford to wait, particularly since he derives satisfaction from the fact that he pays no income tax on the expected gradual enhancement in the real worth of his venturesome capital. In the midst of the developmental process the business man dies. His main source of income—his enterprise as a clothing manufacturer—dries up instantly with his demise. Having to raise two young children, his widow must live economically on the income from investments made up out of the life insurance fund which her husband has provided.

The experimental enterprise yields nothing currently and she cannot afford to wait. Ordinarily such securities can find no ready buyer, and only luck will enable her to sell out her holdings even at a sacrifice and transfer her funds into the senior securities of proven ventures which assure a limited return but promise less than the innovation.

In a rough sense, all securities fall into two broad classes—those that make good and those that wither

[78]

and fade into worthlessness. Individuals endowed with the dubious advantage of hind-sight sometimes feel that, since a particular eight per cent bond carried out all the promises of the borrower, an individual who eschewed the high yielding security and bought instead a Government bond was cheated out of a part of the earning power of his funds.

That assumption is based on delusive reasoning,— it is equivalent to asserting that a man who has insured his house against fire for three years wasted his expenditure if the house failed to burn down during that period. The buying of fire insurance was a recognition that the owner had either to assume the hazard of fire or transfer the risk to an insurance company which would relieve him of all danger of loss for a specified premium. Risk also exists in the realm of securities.

The basic rate on a bond, which in the United States is approximately the last rate paid by the United States Treasury on its new obligations, is rent *for the use of money*. It is the pure interest rate and consists of a reward for the individual who abstains from spending his surplus funds. Let us assume that rate to be four per cent. If that is the basic interest rate, why do certain foreign governments and domestic corporations simultaneously issue bonds bearing six, seven and possibly even eight per cent

[79]

interest? The differential represents primarily a premium to cover the extra risk involved in the fact that the promises of the borrower are less likely to be carried out than are those of the United States Treasury, whose credit represents par.

Sometimes the added risk is potential only and the eight per cent bond pays out, just as the house that is insured against fire may escape the machinations of an incendiary or the hazards of carelessness. Since there is no absolute yardstick for measuring investment risk, the expert buyer of securities, by discriminating among the whole range of possible outlets for surplus funds can find securities which make an undue allowance for the additional risk entailed.

Sometimes the spread in the prices of various bonds reflects prejudice as well as an intelligent weighing of the factors involved. Supply and demand are economic twins which influence the prices of shoes and ships and sealing wax and they also sway the quotations on securities. Sometimes demand is artificially inflated either by waves of popular enthusiasm or by fiats of legislatures. For example, the various states in the United States specify in great detail the kinds of securities that are legal investments for savings banks and trustees. The mere fact that a bond falls under this classification immediately widens its market and tends to raise its price as compared with a security of equal merit which does not happen to fall within the same arbitrary boundaries of the law.

Moreover, certain obviously excellent securities, such as Atchison general 4s, are so frequently recommended by bankers and newspapers that their price reflects their popularity. Furthermore, securities of this type whose worth is appreciated by the expert are in negligible supply, for those who buy them keep them securely tucked away in safe deposit boxes during their whole span of existence.

On the other hand, bonds like the Canadian National Railway issues, which are guaranteed unconditionally as to principal and interest by the Canadian Government, sell at a slightly more advantageous price than they otherwise would because they are not legal investments for savings banks and trustees in New York State and some of the other principal commonwealths. Prejudice and superstition are factors in price too, for market quotations are simply the reflection of the collective financial mind which is occasionally subject to human error.

Many bond buyers dislike a bond selling at a premium because a smaller principal sum is returned when the bond matures than was originally invested. Thus a premium bond of a given corporation frequently sells on a higher and more attractive yield basis than a discount bond of identical character of the same or a similar borrower. The investor who understands his problem each year amortizes (or allows for the eventual wiping out of) the premium and finds a premium bond in every way as desirable, from the investment standpoint, as an obligation acquired below par.

Each intelligent investor must formulate his own program. He himself best knows when to adhere to "safety first" and when to become astutely venturesome.

In the modern scheme of economic affairs the wheels of industry would stop if every buyer of securities confined his purchases exclusively to high grade investments. Risk is inherent in trade, where uncertainties of forthcoming crops and accidental forces such as floods, earthquakes and wars perpetually deflect the normal flowing of the tides of commerce. But, although hazards must be assumed by someone, the risk and dangers of experiment and innovation ought to be undertaken by those qualified to do so. The workingman with only an accumulation of $500 to separate him from poverty, and the widow who would have to lower her standard of living if a few dollars went astray, are obviously not the ones to do so. Risk can best be borne and the

hazards of speculation assumed by those endowed
with sufficient monetary resources and financial in‐
telligence. Individals on the border line who cannot
afford to lose should select securities involving a
minimum of risk.

Generalizations in this field are likely to be of lit‐
tle practical use. Instead in this chapter the spe‐
cific requirements and peculiar needs of different
classes in the community will be analyzed. Defi‐
nite suggestions of suitable stocks and bonds for
men and women of all degrees of wealth and affluence
will be made, but the reader is cautioned to check
up on the desirability of individual securities at the
time of investing in the light of altered conditions.
The recommendations made in this chapter are based
on conditions at the time of this writing. However
since finance like all human institutions is subject to
the law of flux, prudent investors should regularly
take inventories of their holdings and examine their
worth in the light of fluctuating economic conditions.

I

How the Workingman should Invest his Funds

Relatively high wages in the United States, es‐
pecially during periods of prosperity, should enable
the wage earner to save at least a small share of the

contents of his weekly pay envelope. The working-man's thrift fund represents part of the fruits of past labor saved up for future enjoyment—or use. It is the margin which would save him and his family from being dispossessed of their home in case of unemployment, caused either by general economic conditions or by illness or misfortune. It is the small fund which would assure adequate medical attention for the children in case of illness. It is, in short, the small stake of the ordinary individual in the colossal wealth of the United States. It is a fund to be nurtured carefully at the outset and protected for the legitimate uses of the workingman and his family.

In selecting investments the wage earner, who, presumably, is untrained in the ways of finance, should set out to attain primarily safety of principal and assured regularity of income.

Any conscientious banker or competent financial editor of a reputable newspaper is always glad to give impartial and intelligent advice to the new investor. But they are less dramatic and less emotional in their approach and less extravagant in their promises than a whole corps of vicious and dishonest self-seeking fakers who, unable to allure funds from the financially literate man of affairs, make their facile and vicious fortunes from misleading men and women of

[84]

small means. The Ponzis, the "Doc" Cooks, the Pandolfos, and even the more subtle tricksters and swindlers of finance promise or suggest huge returns from small investments.

Anything can happen in this world of infinite possibilities, but the record of statisticians of promotions shows that the mortality rate of such new ventures is inordinately high. High yields and speculative promises are signposts indicating danger. Any securities yielding more than the current return on United States Government bonds entail additional risk. Some of the better grade and better known government securities, however, are for all practical purposes safe and suitable even for individuals in quest primarily of safety.

It has become relatively easy for the workingman to get sound advice as to what securities he should buy. A more difficult problem is that of controlling dangerous impulses, extravagant tendencies and slovenly habits in his own household.

Thrift is seldom likely to be effective unless it becomes automatic. It is better to save a dollar a week, for example, than two or three dollars one week and nothing the next. Man is a creature of habit and psychologists agree that good habits can become as much a part of the automatic equipment of an individual as bad tendencies.

Funds accumulating with unbroken regularity increase with amazing rapidity. The compound interest table does more spectacular things than the ordinary promoter can ever hope to achieve. *For example, if a workingman should buy a sound six per cent bond to-day and reinvest his interest regularly his principal would double itself in less than twelve years.*

Investments represent labor saved up. The individual who lives from hand to mouth is rushing inevitably toward personal bankruptcy and ruin. He is failing to make provision, in accordance with modern accounting practice, for depletion and depreciation of his physical machine which, like everything else, is certain to run down and become impaired eventually. Every corporation sets up reserves against the unavoidable wearing out of its equipment. The intelligent individual does the same by laying aside a definite portion of his annual earnings as a fund to finance his retirement to take care of him at a time when natural or premature inefficiency overtakes him and he lacks the capacity to stand up as he does at present in the relentless competition of the workaday world.

If the workingman had a definite contract with the Almighty as to the duration of his stay on earth he might conceivably find acceptable substitutes for life insurance. But, since at any moment a thoughtless taxi driver or a streak of lightning may terminate his stay on this planet, his only certain means of building up a fund to take care of his dependents after his departure is insurance. Stripped of nonsense and selling talk, insurance is nothing more than a collective scheme which turns the great gamble of the span of an individual life into the statistical certainty of the expectancy of a large group.

Life insurance should be the first consideration. Unless the individual can afford the luxury of frills, the ordinary life policy is always the most attractive. A savings bank account which represents a share in a diversified collection of high-grade investments should come next. Though the yield is only four per cent the element of safety is high and the fund can ordinarily be immediately drawn upon in case of emergency.

Building and loan shares which offer a means of saving a definite amount each month and which also facilitate the ownership of a home, are convenient vehicles of thrift for the individual of small means who in this way can accumulate systematically in amounts from a dollar a month upwards.

Automatic saving is made possible by a number

of corporations which, in order to create more human relationships with their workers give them especially convenient opportunities to acquire ownership shares of the business for which they work. Many corporations, in order to help their employees get on in the world, arrange to divert a small part of the weekly pay into a fund by which the individual acquires part ownership of his employer's business. The sociological advantages of such an arrangement, in so far as it stimulates the interest of the worker in his daily task and humanizes the relationship between employer and employee, make it desirable for the worker to tie up at least a small part of his capital in such stock provided it is sound.

However, ordinarily such arrangements are only for the acquisition of common stock, too much of which would weaken the investment structure of the worker who ought to have a large proportion of his funds in higher grade securities, particularly since an acute depression might not only deprive him of his job but of dividends on the stock of his employer at the same time. A principle of investment safety is diversification, which means scattering thrift funds in various localities and various types of economic activities so that if perchance one goes wrong the others are likely to remain solid.

Except for shares of the company for which he

works, the workingman, as a general rule, should eschew all stocks and bonds which are even moderately speculative. He should shun promotions and untried schemes. He should select primarily sound bonds and perhaps a few preferred stocks and should buy them through his savings bank, commercial bank or through a broker recommended either by a banker or some other impartial individual equally competent to pass upon the ethics and financial standing of the broker.[1]

The following list, plus life, insurance epitomizes the foregoing investment suggestions for the workingman. The investment of $300 in each of the following seven bonds, and $200 in each of the preferred stocks, would give an annual yield of $162 [2] on an investment of $3,100.

Bonds

United States Treasury 4¼s   1952
Guaranteed First Mortgages

[1] See Chap. XII, "How to Select an Honest Broker."

[2] The return on the investment in this and other lists in this chapter is figured on the basis of prevailing prices in the middle of August 1924. Readers can ascertain current quotations from the daily newspaper, and are cautioned that this list and others in this chapter are intended merely to illustrate the general principles involved. They are not intended as suggestions suitable for all individuals in perpetuity. The investor, desiring to act on these recommendations in subsequent years, should check up on the current conditions of the companies mentioned.

Common Sense of Money and Investments

Building and Loan Shares
Canadian Pacific Debenture 4s
New York Central Refunding and Improvement 5s 2013
Niagara Falls Power 5s   1932
Chicago Union Station 6½s   1963

Stocks

United States Steel 7% preferred
National Biscuit Company 7% preferred
Western Electric Company 7% preferred
Atchison, Topeka and Sante Fe, 5% preferred
New York Telephone 6½% preferred

II

How Widows and Orphans Should Invest their Capital

In the encyclopedia of bunk, on which the financial propagandist draws heavily for his inspiration, much appears about injustice to the widow and orphan. Every time a legislator arises to wreak vengeance on a corporation entity, the chorus of defenders of things-as-they-are clamors loudly about the poor widows and orphans who will suffer from unwarranted punitive efforts. Of course, if well advised, widows and orphans will avoid speculative securities which are sensitive to the ebb and flow of commerce and the influence of politicians. Such immunity from the hazards to which all business is subject can be attained only in a relative sense.

Lord Leverhulme, British soap manufacturer and one of the wealthiest individuals in the Old World, is an orphan and Mrs. Russell Sage was a widow. But in the sense in which the problem is here treated, securities will be selected suitable for widows and orphans of limited financial resources. Crooks and charlatans eagerly read the death notices in newspapers and are on the alert to separate unfortunate widows and orphans from their bequests.

Forced to live on the return from a relatively small supply of capital, the widow and orphan are beset with temptations to attain the largest yield consistent with safety. But the person in this class should remember that, generally speaking, the degree of safety declines as the yield rises. A security promising a high return, which, in human terms, might mean a few luxuries and greater comfort, might in reality bring about the loss of principal which would ruthlessly cut down the standard of living. Tragic experience over a long period of years has revealed that it is a good policy for the widow and orphan, un-

[91]

tutored in the ways of business, to select primarily high grade securities. Those stocks which represent little more than the aspirations, hopes and hot air of speculative promoters are not for individuals in these economic circumstances.

Liberty bonds are the ideal security for persons in this category and after them the underlying obligations of the most ably managed domestic railroads, industrial and public utility corporations.

The following list is suggested. The investment of $400 in each of the following bonds, and $400 in each of the following preferred stocks would give a yield of $237.84 annually on an investment of $4,800.

Bonds

First Liberty 4¼s	1947
Guaranteed First Mortgages	
Union Pacific Refunding 4s	2008
Pennsylvania Railroad General 4½s	1965
United States Steel Sinking Fund 5s	1963
Canadian Government 5s	1952
United Kingdom 5½s	1937
New York Telephone 6s	1941
Province of Ontario 5s	1942

Stocks

General Electric Special
United States Steel preferred
Union Pacific Railway preferred

[92]

Investment Programs for Rich and Poor

III

How Clerks and Other Salaried Workers Should Invest their Savings

The white-collared worker, whose income is frequently no larger than that of the man in overalls, faces a slightly different problem, for he is frequently in a somewhat better position in respect to financial judgment and information. His education and practical experience have better fitted him intelligently to follow the trend of business conditions which affect the value of securities. He can, therefore, legitimately hold securities entailing a moderately higher degree of risk than one to whom the current symbols of finance offer no clue as to the meaning of trade cycles and their effect on the intrinsic worth of stocks and bonds.

Moreover, there is ordinarily greater stability to the employment of the clerk, the bookkeeper, the secretary, the file clerk and the junior executive than to that of the workingman whose fate in times of depression is frequently unemployment. The clerical classes in building up their thrift fund are frequently misled by false interpretation of stray gossip picked up during the daily routine. A conversation overheard, a chance remark from a department head or the tip of a fellow clerk frequently are allowed to determine his financial program instead of an intelligent analysis of his own needs and the surest methods of attaining his goal. Inside information which at best is fraught with hazard may be of some use to the speculator, but to the investor who is in quest, not of appreciation of his capital, but rather of safety of principal and regularity of income, it is likely to be of little assistance.

The following list is suggested. The investment of $400 in each of the following bonds and $200 in each of the following stocks would give a yield of $274.16 on an investment of $5,200.

Bonds

First Liberty 4¼s	1947
United States Treasury 4¼s	1947–1952
Building and Loan Association	
Delaware & Hudson first 4s	1943
Southern Pacific-Frisco Terminal 4s	1950
Montana Power 5s	1943
New England Telephone Company 5s	1952
Swiss Government 8s	1940
Cleveland, Cincinnati, Chicago & St. Louis 6s	1929

Stocks

Consolidated Gas of New York Preferred
New York Telephone 6½ preferred
Corn Products 7% preferred
American Car & Foundry 7% preferred
Illinois Central 6% preferred

Investment Programs for Rich and Poor

Niagara Falls Power 7% preferred
American Telephone & Telegraph
Atchison, Topeka & Santa Fe common

IV

How a Small Business Man Should Invest His Savings

The small business man assumes the hazards of trade in his own enterprise and is in that sense a commercial speculator. In building up an independent array of investment securities on which he can draw in case of trouble in his own business or in case of emergency in his family, he should select securities of a high grade.

For his purposes ready marketability and a high collateral value are important considerations. On short notice he may need additional cash for his business or personal expenditures and he must have securities which can be quickly realized upon either through sale at the market place or by means of a loan secured by the stocks and bonds at the bank. Therefore, he should have among his holdings a large proportion of issues which are listed in the New York Stock Exchange or which have a ready market over the counter. Lacking ready salability, otherwise sound securities might be unsuited to his peculiar needs.

Moreover, since he is speculating in his own busi-

[95]

ness, he has little to gain in placing his thrift funds at the disposal of other speculators at the heads of corporations whose securities are sold to the public. Instead he should seek primarily safe bonds and the best grade of preferred stocks. Finance as conducted at present constitutes a highly specialized activity and the fact that the small business man has made a success in his local butcher shop or grocery store, is no indication that he can succeed in outguessing the professional traders and insiders to whom speculation in stocks is a regular business.

The following list is suggested. The investment of $300 in each of the following stocks and bonds would give a yield of $256.23 each year on $4,500.

Bonds

Liberty First 4¼s	1933–1938
United States Treasury 4¼s	1947–1952
New York Edison 6½s	1941
Canadian Northern 6½s	1946
Chesapeake & Ohio Railroad General 4½s	1992
Dutch East Indies 6s	1947
Kingdom of Sweden 6s	1939
Southern California Edison General Refunding 5s	1944

Stocks

Endicott-Johnson 7% preferred
Western Electric 7% preferred

[96]

Investment Programs for Rich and Poor

Chesapeake & Ohio 6½% preferred
American Telephone & Telegraph
Brooklyn Edison common
United States Steel common
New York Central common

V

How a Business Man Should Invest his Surplus Funds

An investment scheme is the means by which the business man can avoid putting all his eggs in one basket. The successful individual who controls an enterprise as sole proprietor sometimes will want to increase his outside holdings relatively, and at other stages of the business cycle will desire to draw funds from his investments for his business needs. At other times seeing danger signs ahead in business he will strive to reduce his inventories, turning merchandise into cash which will go temporarily into sound outside investments.

For a fund which can be quickly drawn on when required a high degree of marketability of securities is essential. For balance sheet purposes, securities are only one stage removed from cash on hand and should be such as can be immediately sold at the stock market or used as collateral for bank loans. Incidentally the banks will ordinarily make col-

[97]

lateral loans only on securities which are listed on a stock exchange and regularly quoted in the newspapers.

For his secondary investment needs—consisting of surplus funds which his own business is not likely to need—the business man's expert knowledge of economic conditions enables him to hold securities bearing a larger element of risk than so-called high grade issues. For example, he can consistently acquire in times of approaching prosperity stocks whose dividends depend on current earning power and get rid of them when he sees indications of an approaching depression. Every prosperous business man, however, is not necessarily a shrewd reader of the financial weather reports and, if he lacks the capacity for detecting approaching economic storms, he should concentrate mainly on securities whose earning power continues even during recession.

The following list is suggested. The investment of $1,000 in each of the following bonds and stocks would give a yield of $975.40 on an investment of $17,000.

Bonds

First Liberty 4¼s	1947
United States Treasury 4¼s	1947–1952
New York Telephone 6s	1941

Investment Programs for Rich and Poor

Pere-Marquette First 5s	1956
Southern Railway First 5s	1994
Great Northern 7s	1936
Kingdom of Norway 6s	1952
Standard Oil of New York 6½s	1933
Bell Telephone of Pennsylvania 5s	1948

Stocks

May Company preferred
General Motors 7% preferred
New York, Chicago & St. Louis preferred
Union Pacific common
American Telephone & Telegraph
Liggett & Myers Tobacco
Westinghouse Electric & Manufacturing common
American Car & Foundry common

VI

How the Business Woman Should Invest her Surplus Funds

Woman's financial place is in the safest of investments, according to the Wall Street credo. A now defunct brokerage house which circumstances compelled to assert its high morals used to boast that it would not accept accounts from women. Thus, despite the demonstration of the obvious by capable women bank officials and bond sellers, the traditional investment adviser continues to associate women with imbeciles and minors.

[99]

Common Sense of Money and Investments

Sex should be no factor in selecting investments. Risk should be assumed in proportion as the security buyer is financially and intellectually able to undertake the hazard.

Each individual investment problem should be decided on its own merits, and those in quest of advice should describe the special facts which condition their requirements. But, in the name of the sovereign female voters of the country, let the financial world realize that some women are better equipped with capital and brains to accept higher yielding securities than innumerable men. The theory was so long held that woman's place was outside the Stock Exchange that men naturally understood the workings of speculative machinery better than women.

Entirely aside from questions of sex, only the specially gifted should seek to risk the dangers of speculation. Irrespective of whether widows or orphans, the vast majority of folk would do better to invest in sound bonds than in alluring yet evanescent stocks. Decisions in such matters, however, should be made without regard to race, creed, color or previous condition of servitude. By her intelligent adaptation to the modern financial and business world the modern woman has compelled candid observers to answer in the affirmative Alice Duer Miller's inquiry, "Are Women People?"

[100]

Investment Programs for Rich and Poor

The old superstition that it was sinful to sell a woman anything more hazardous than a United States Government bond is fast vanishing. For the woman who reads the financial pages of well edited newspapers and who earns her living in the illuminating give and take of commerce is capable of holding a more diversified list of investments. However, she should lay the foundation of her investment structure with solid rocks consisting of securities of the highest grade. Bonds with a slightly smaller degree of safety and good preferred stocks may be acquired later.

For the woman of financial training who has sufficient leisure to keep in touch with her holdings, the following list is suggested. The investment of $500 in each of the following stocks and bonds gives a yield of $394.50 on an investment of $7,000.

Bonds

First Liberty 4¼s	1947
United States Treasury 4¼s	1947–1952
Canadian Northern 7s	1940
Atlantic Coast Line first 4s	1952
Humble Oil 5s	1932

Stocks

Consolidated Gas 6% participating preferred
Endicott-Johnson 7% preferred
Chesapeake & Ohio 6½% preferred

American Tobacco 6% preferred
Pere-Marquette 5% prior preference
American Telephone & Telegraph
Atchison, Topeka & Santa Fe common
Brooklyn Edison common
Western Union common

VII

How the Teacher and Minister should Invest their Savings

The vocations of leading men out of the purgatory of ignorance and of pointing out to adults and children alike the sundry roads to paradise are far removed from the throbbing excitement of the market place. Accordingly, many intelligent members of the learned professions paradoxically enough are easy prey for venders of gold bricks and hot air. Sucker lists are generously studded with D. D.'s and Ph. D.'s.

Too many unprosperous teachers and ministers, whose income is to a large extent psychical and only partly financial, think that escape from a life of drudgery and economy is to be found through acting on the suggestive fairy tales of promoters of wildcat oil companies, mines that probably never will be worked, and tire companies that produce only inflated selling talk.

[102]

Investment Programs for Rich and Poor

Men and women of these professions who are ordinarily without specialized financial or business experience should buy only securities of the higher grades. Life insurance and annuities should form a conspicuous part of the investment program of the teacher and minister. Various beneficial organizations serve the teaching and clerical professions, sometimes at a lower figure than ordinary commercial companies. The Carnegie Foundation provides pensions for certain groups of teachers after the retirement age.

Besides the foregoing, the following list is suggested. The investment of $500 in each of the following bonds and stocks would yield $408 annually on an investment of $8,000.

Bonds

First Liberty 4¼s	1947
United States Treasury 4¼s	1947–1952
Guaranteed First Mortgages	
Union Pacific First 4s	1947
New York Telephone 4½s	1939
United Kingdom 5½s	1937
Canadian Northern 6½s	1946
Toronto Harbor 4½s	1953
P. Lorillard 5s	1951

Stocks

National Lead 7% preferred
National Biscuit 7% preferred

United States Steel 7% preferred
General Electric Special 6% stock
Western Electric 7% preferred
National Bank of Commerce stock
Bankers' Trust Company stock

VIII

How Physicians and Dentists should Invest their Savings

Security fakers act on the theory that experts in physiology and medicine are mere innocent babes in the realm of investment finance. Physicians and dentists as a class have been the special prey of illegitimate stock promoters of every kind.

Like medicine, finance is a highly specialized field. The physician or dentist who disposes of his surplus funds without expert advice is perhaps only a degree less foolish than the layman who removes his own appendix or extracts his own ulcerated tooth.

Unlike the business man who can turn the fruits of his prosperity back into his own enterprise, the physician or dentist must necessarily seek outside fields for investment. Only a limited portion of his earnings can be profitably placed in books, and surgical instruments. After paying his family expenses and for his nurses and clerical help and pro-

[104]

viding his office equipment, the medical man of large income necessarily must take a part in financing the activities of Governments and in providing the monetary sinews of great railroad, public utility and industrial corporations. He will do this job of investing wisely if he carries over into this new field his scientific training and spirit of analysis. On the other hand, he will err, as so many physicians and dentists do, if he places his surplus funds in securities carelessly recommended by a patient who brings so-called inside information into the doctor's office.

Irrespective of his financial condition neither the physician nor the dentist can consistently participate in the thrills and dangers of margin speculation. [3] It is destructive of confidence and professional dignity for a medical man to leave his patient in the midst of an examination to answer the telephone call from a broker shouting for more margin or announcing a profit or disseminating a new red-hot tip on the market.

Reason and the peculiar requirements of the profession alike make it desirable for the physician to concentrate on securities which do not require him to hang over the stock ticker for five hours during every business day.

[3] See Chap. XV for an explanation of margin trading.

Common Sense of Money and Investments

The physician's earning power furthermore stops with death or when disease overtakes him. He has created no independent entity such as a manufacturing enterprise or a retail store such as the business man forges, which can continue to yield returns after the founder has retired. The physician and the dentist must therefore provide for their old age, for their physical incapacities and for their dependents through adequate life, health and accident insurance and sound investments.

The following list is suggested. The investment of $500 in each of the following bonds and stocks gives an annual yield of $366.80 on an investment of $7,000.

Bonds

First Liberty 4¼s	1947
United States Treasury 4¼s	1947–1952
Chicago Union Station 5s	1963
Virginia Railway 5s	1962
Southern California Edison 5s	1944
Pennsylvania General 4½s	1965
Atlantic Coast Line 4½s	1964

Stocks

Atchison, Topeka and Santa Fe Railway preferred
Union Pacific preferred
R. J. Reynolds Tobacco preferred
Western Electric preferred
Niagara Falls Power preferred

[106]

Investment Programs for Rich and Poor

Western Electric preferred
National Biscuit preferred

IX

How the Farmer should Invest his Surplus Funds

Whereas the physician and dentist and the school teacher and ministers have been especially easy urban victims of security charlatans, fake promoters have by no means found their best hunting grounds in the cities. Out in the country districts the farmer, thinking of the great factory centers—largely as mental abstractions—has long been ready to believe assurances of itinerant stock salesmen that purchase of their offerings would enable the rustic classes to participate generously in the fabulously large earnings of the great industries of the towns. The stock selling gentry act on the belief that the ordinary tiller of the soil knows little about business save that which relates to the condition of crops and herds.

The excitement that comes with dreams of quick profits and easy wealth makes suckers in every walk of economic life and the farmer has not been alone in his financial misadventures. However, in periods of prosperity venders of worthless but neatly engraved certificates of stock have taken enormous tribute from the American tillers of the soil.

Far removed from the tickers and the other sources

of information, the farmer should not load up with securities which require incessant watching. The radio, the telephone and the rural free delivery bring him nearer than ever before to the centers of urban life, but adequate care of his crops requires his personal attention and his absence from brokerage offices.

The farmer who is improving the standard of living of his family needs a stabilized income. Sending his sons and daughters to far-away colleges and providing for travel for his family and for the upkeep of pleasure automobiles require an unvarying income. Once a farmer has embarked on a career of imitating the ways of city folk, he cannot conveniently step down in times of small yielding crops. Yet he is able to obtain no guaranties from Mother Nature that the rains and conditions of the soil shall always contribute equally to his luxury fund. Joseph, in ancient Egypt, was the first to enunciate the principle of the agriculture business cycle when he discovered the more or less unscientific, yet suggestive, formula that seven lean years follow seven fat years in the granaries of the world. Recognizing the fluctuating status of his crops, the farmer should in periods of unusual prosperity build up an investment fund on which he can draw during periods of recession.

Investment Programs for Rich and Poor

For this purpose, the following securities are suggested. The investment of $1,000 in each of the following bonds and stocks would give an annual yield of $786.50 on an investment of $15,000.

Bonds

First Liberty 4¼s	1947
United States Treasury 4¼s	1947–1952
Guaranteed First Mortgages	
United Kingdom 5½s	1937
Delaware & Hudson 5½s	1937
Chicago, Burlington & Quincy 5s	1971
New York Telephone 4½s	1939
Dominion of Canada 5s	1952
Canadian Northern 6½s	1946
Chicago Union Station 5s	1963

Stocks

National Biscuit 7% preferred
United States Steel 7% preferred
Niagara Falls Power 7% preferred
National Lead 7% preferred
American Telephone & Telegraph

X

How Trustees should Invest Funds Placed in their Care

The process of investing on the part of the trustee is ordinarily more automatic than that of other securities buyers, for, unless he is expressly permitted to do otherwise he must confine his purchases to a certain type of securities specified by state law which are legally eligible for such purposes and are assumed to involve the minimum of speculative risk.

Bonds of the United States and of every state in the Union with the exception of Virginia are legal investments in New York State. Moreover, obligations of municipalities are considered to be eligible trustee's investments provided the state in which the municipality is situated entered the union before 1869, that the town or city itself has been incorporated for twenty-five years and that the total debt is held within definitely defined limits. Railroad first mortgages are generally considered legal for trustees, if the road in question has earned and paid a dividend of at least four per cent on its entire capital outstanding for the past five years.

First mortgages on real property with the state of New York are legal investments provided the amount of mortgage does not exceed two thirds of the assessed valuation of the property. Obligations of the Federal Land Banks are legal for trustees, but with a few exceptions the obligations of individual joint stock banks do not come within the class of trustees' investments in the Empire State.

Competent trustees, however, do not blindly select

legal bonds. Even the carefully defined requirements for legal investments in New York State have
permitted bonds of less than the best grade to remain
on the eligible list. For example, the obligations
of certain railroads have remained legal, although
as a result of shifting economic conditions they no
longer comply with the spirit of the lawmakers.
Eventually, however, such bonds are stricken from
the list of legals unless the borrowers recover their
original financial strength.

The following is a list of bonds considered legal
for the investment of trust funds in New York. An
investment of $28,000 in this list gives an annual re-
turn of $1,159.20.

First Liberty 4¼s	1947
United States Treasury 4¼s	1947–1952
New York City 4½s	1957
New Jersey 5s	1961
Detroit, Michigan 4½s	1942
State of North Carolina 4½s	1962
San Francisco, California 5s	1946
Federal Land Bank 5s	1941
Illinois Central 3½s	1951
Northern Pacific 6s	2047
Atchison, Topeka & Santa Fe General 4s	1995
Central Railroad of New Jersey General 5s	1987
Union Pacific 4s	1947
New York Central Refunding and Improve-
ment 5s	2013

XI

How Associations should Invest Funds on Hand

Treasurers of voluntary associations, such as hospitals, clubs and fraternal orders are confronted with nearly the same problem as those in charge of so-called trust funds. However, they are not by law restricted to the specified investments legal for trustees. A voluntary association is ordinarily free to place its money in any type of securities its responsible officers desire, but they should, for reasons of prudence, select only high grade issues.

The ordinary association makes annual budgets and its officers contract for expenses in the belief that the expected income will be available. If part of the fund should be in speculative securities it would be entirely likely that dividends would be suspended during times of depression and the officers of the organization would find themselves unable to meet obligations already undertaken. A portion of the funds should be in cash as a deposit in an ordinary commercial or savings bank subject to immediate call and funds which will be needed at a definite time in the future a few months hence should be placed in United States Treasury certificates of indebtedness or prime bankers' acceptances, which can be quickly converted into cash without any depreciation of principal.

For more permanent investment, the following securities are suggested. The investment of $1,000 in each of the following bonds gives a yield of $474 on an investment of $10,000.

First Liberty 4¼s	1947
United States Treasury 4¼s	1947–1952
New York City 4s	1957
Guaranteed First Mortgages	
New York Telephone 6s	1941
Canadian Northern 7s	1940
Canadian Government 5s	1952
New York Edison 6½s	1941
Province of Ontario 5s	1942
New York Central Refunding and Improvement 5s	2013

XII

How a Corporation should Invest its Surplus Funds

Wisely managed corporations, ready for a period of adversity on the one hand, or an era of unexpected expansion on the other, keep a part of their surplus in cash and in liquid securities which can quickly be converted into ready money.

In buying securities for a corporation, the officers usually have in mind one of two objectives; First, to

[113]

build up a secondary reserve which can be drawn on in case of need; and, secondly, for reasons of business policy, to acquire securities of companies in the same or related business for purposes of control or at any rate closer contact. Where the motive is to link up into inter-corporate relationships with probable customers or competitors, the problem is not purely an investment question.

Where the only motive is to place idle funds in interest-bearing securities, the element of time during which the funds will be available is often the determining factor in the selection of securities. If the surplus will be needed within twelve months or less, the highest type of short-term securities, such as United States Government certificates of indebtedness, prime bankers' acceptances and high grade commercial paper will be most available. For longer time funds Liberty bonds, high grade railroad first mortgage bonds and other issues of the best grade are suitable.

The investment of $2,000 in each of the following items would yield $1,245 annually on an investment of $30,000.

Commercial Paper
Prime Bankers Acceptances
United States Treasury Certificates of Indebtedness

Investment Programs for Rich and Poor

United States Treasury notes	1924–1927
First Liberty 4¼s	1947
United States Treasury 4¼s	1947–1952
Chicago, Burlington & Quincy Equipment-Trust Certificate 6s	1933–1935
Michigan Central Equipment-Trust Certificate 6s	1923–1935
Virginia Railway Equipment-Trust Certificate 6s	1924–1935
Southern Railway Equipment-Trust Certificate 6s	1924–1935
Dominion of Canada 5s	1952
New York City 4s	1957
Niagara Falls Power First 5s	1932
Pennsylvania General 4½s	1965
Union Pacific First and Refunding 4s	2008

XIII

How Commercial Banks should Invest their Surplus Funds

The ordinary commercial bank is the largest debtor in the community, and its debt consists mainly of demand obligations to depositors. Accordingly, its investments must be in large measure those which can almost immediately be converted into cash when required. Liquidity, which involves ready marketability, is a prime essential for bank investments. Furthermore, since the banker is dealing mainly with other people's money, that of the business enterprises

[115]

and the individuals of the community who entrust their funds to him for safe-keeping, it is essential that he place the bank's funds in high grade investments where the danger of loss is negligible.

One of the bank's primary functions is to take care of the legitimate credit needs of its own customers and thus provide the funds for financing the ordinary commerce of its own community. Afterwards, the bank can legitimately place funds in call loans against stocks and bonds and acceptances which can be arranged through its New York correspondents, and in commercial paper, acceptances, and treasury certificates of indebtedness maturing in three to six months.

It is well to give preference, in buying commercial paper, to that which is eligible for rediscount with the Federal Reserve Bank, thus providing an immediate cash reserve. In selecting investments of longer maturity, the bank should buy only issues of the highest grade, which ordinarily fluctuate less in market value than inferior securities. Although the commercial bank is not restricted to securities, which are legal for savings banks and trustees, its holdings are frequently checked by national and state bank examiners. Securities are ordinarily carried on the bank's books at either cost or market value, whichever happens to be lower.

[116]

Investment Programs for Rich and Poor

The following list is suggested for banks. The investment of $3,000 in each of the following securities gives a yield of $1,765.60 on an investment of $42,000.

Commercial Paper	
Prime Bankers' Acceptances	
United States Treasury Certificates	
United States Treasury notes	1924–1927
First Liberty 4¼s	1947
United States Treasury 4¼s	1947–1952
Canadian Pacific Equipment-Trust Certificate 6s	1923–1932
Illinois Central Equipment-Trust Certificate 5½s	1926–1938
Louisville & Nashville Equipment-Trust Certificate 6s	1925–1936
Union Pacific Refunding 4s	2008
Southern Pacific Refunding 4s	1955
United Kingdom 5½s	1937
Dominion of Canada 5s	1952
United States Steel Sinking Fund 5s	1963

CHAPTER XI

WHEN TO SWITCH FROM STOCKS TO BONDS

How Business Cycles Affect the Investor.

Rich investors often believe "eternal vigilance is the price of safety." John D. Rockefeller maintains a regularly organized bureau which employs shrewd analysts who are continually on the lookout for security bargains or advantageous switches from one issue to another.— THOMAS GIBSON.

IN modern business, there is a perpetual ebbing and flowing of the tides. Economists who have studied these habits of flux have described the process as a business cycle, the various phases of which include a revival of activity, intense prosperity, a crisis, and a depression.

Popular thinking about the vicissitudes of commerce in terms of the cycle theory is at the moment at a peak of popularity. The view that the seeds of prosperity are sown in a period of depression and vice versa is a helpful aid to envisaging changes in a broad perspective. In so far as the business cycle theory is truly understood (as a description of the average flow of events between hard times and good times in leading industrial countries) it facilitates reasoning about elusive trade facts. When, however, as frequently occurs, the layman ascribes to the theory the universality of Newton's law of gravitation or of Einstein's deductions regarding relativity, it is high time for some one to urge that the alleged freedom of the will has some bearing on the struggle of mankind to make a living. Those who misunderstand the business cycle theory resignedly feel that nothing in the power of man can either hasten prosperity or delay severe recessions.

The contrary is nearer the truth. As the view that more or less definite cycles follow one another in the world of give and take is more widely accepted, the mere knowledge will tend to lessen the intensity of the changes. The more astute men of business attempt to anticipate changes, and this tendency to discount adjustments in advance in turn spreads the disposition to change over a longer period of time— flattening the peaks and the depressions. Every serious attempt to make known to the enterprising public the real facts regarding current business checks in a small way the wideness of the swings between changing phases.

In 1913, Dr. Wesley Clair Mitchell wrote his classic work on "Business Cycles," (published by the University of California), which now unhappily is out of print, and crystallized American thought on the subject. In the upswing of the war period, relatively little attention was paid to abstract reasoning, but during the setback subsequently and the beginnings of a revival later the theory came into new vogue. Many explanations of business cycles had been made by earlier writers. A business cycle theory was set forth in the Bible, which taught that there would be seven fat years followed by seven lean years. Of course, the business of the speculator who assumes the risks of business, is to anticipate these shifts of the favoring winds.

The Mitchell theory is "a descriptive analysis of the processes of cumulative change by which a revival of activity develops into intense prosperity, by which this prosperity engenders a crisis, by which crisis turns into depression, and by which depression, after growing more severe for a time, finally leads to such a revival of activity as that with which the cycle began."

The economic situation in America after the war was in many ways unprecedented, and any observer who tried to explain it wholly in terms of the past was inevitably headed toward a precipice. And yet in the subsequent period of business recovery, after the severe slump of 1920 culminating in the attainment of the most depressed speculative prices in August 1921, many elements correspond roughly with the conditions of this phase of a theoretical cycle as described by Dr. Mitchell.

To take advantage of all the phases of a business cycle, the holder of securities would have to shift his securities from time to time.

He would buy common shares at a tail end of a period of depression and hold them during a time of revival and sell them well on toward the close of an era of high prosperity. Then he would keep his funds in highly liquid form, such as bankers' acceptances or short term notes, ready to buy sound bonds in time of depression, during which receding money rates would tend to support the market value of his bonds at times when shares, discounting adversity, would tumble in market worth.

With interest rates mounting at such a period some operators find it advisable for a time to keep their funds especially liquid so that they can observe changes and be in a position instantly to act after having reached a decision. They thus either keep their funds unprofitably idle at the bank, or invest them in high grade bankers' acceptances or in call loans at the New York Stock Exchange.

Efforts to take advantage of all the vast fluctuations of an inefficiently geared industrial system, whose ebb and flow are a source of injury to the many, would involve also subtler switches from long term to short term bonds and at other phases of the cycle from one type of stock to another.

CHAPTER XII

HOW TO SELECT AN HONEST BROKER

Separating the Wheat from the Chaff.

The broker is the connecting link between buyers and sellers. He is one who negotiates sales or contracts as an agent. The word is old. The early English form was "broceur." By some it is believed to be derived from the Saxon word "broc," which meant misfortune, and the first brokers indeed appear to have been men who failed in business as principals and have been compelled to pick up a precarious living as agents.—SERENO S. PRATT.

AN investor rarely buys securities directly from another investor. He almost invariably makes purchases or sales through an intermediary—a broker or investment dealer. It is of paramount importance to select a middle man of probity and financial responsibility. A bucketeer, who swindles customers instead of serving them, can turn a Liberty bond purchase into as unprofitable a transaction as the buying of worthless "blue sky" stocks.

A reputable broker is a definite asset for the investor. He not only executes orders quickly and at a low fee, but also supplements this service with advice and with information regarding securities. On the other hand, a dishonest broker is bent on separating his customers from their money. An honest investment dealer may give advice which proves unfortunate, but his intention is to serve in a way which will prove profitable to his customers. His chief profit comes from commissions, which he makes whether the customer succeeds or fails. A successful customer will remain a permanent one, giving future orders, whereas the failures pass quickly out of sight.

It is no easy matter for the layman to separate the sheep from the goats in the financial world. Exquisite mahogany furniture and extravagant rugs are devices frequently employed by the unworthy to impress strangers with their solidity and responsibility. Appearances constitute a poor guide to reliability. Good advice would be: *Never buy or sell securities through a strange broker without making an independent check on his integrity.*

If an individual lacks the capacity for judging a broker, he would do well to buy his securities directly through a bank, which in turn acts through a broker. Most banks, as a matter of service, will arrange to help their customers judge a broker's standing. The larger institutions have card indexes of the morals and methods of a wide number of brokers, and have a record of their vices and virtues. Moreover, through subscriptions to Proudfoot's and Bishop's services, which keep tabs on brokers, the banks are able to supplement their own information. The smaller banks are able to draw upon the information of the larger.

Certain banks, particularly outside of New York, had been careless in the past in giving recommendations. They sometimes assess the worth of men according to their bank balances instead of in accordance with their ethics. In recent years, there has been a tendency toward improvement in this direction. The laws of slander and the desire to keep out of trouble have tended to make bankers cautious in expressing opinions about the unworthy. Therefore, unless you have confidential relations with a banker, it would be well to phrase your question in such a way that the banker can set you right without assuming undue risk. For example, ask: "Shall I buy my securities through John Smith, or would you suggest some one else who is, in your opinion, entirely worthy of my confidence?"

Fly-by-nights, who have their offices under their hats, are known to the guardians of reputable stock exchanges, and are denied admission to the organized market places. The New York Stock Exchange has no monopoly of virtue and some of its members have offended, but membership in that exchange is a presumption in favor of a broker because the rules of that organization help to protect the public. Membership in the principal out-of-town exchanges is a good sign also. The lesser New York exchanges have been raising their standards of membership recently, and some of their members are worthy of trust.

Some of the large reputable bond houses do not belong to the exchanges, because they do no stock business. Their independence is in no sense a reflection on their standing. Many of such unaffiliated houses, however, belong to the Investment Bankers' Association of America, an organization which is very jealous of its good name and which sedulously seeks to exclude from membership crooks and charlatans.

The press is another potential guide to good houses. Some newspapers have been and still are careless of their responsibility, and in using the advertising columns of newspapers the reader must show discrimination.

CHAPTER XIII

HOW TO DETECT A SECURITY CHARLATAN

Characteristics of Blue Sky Promoters

This country has been deluged with "Blue Sky Laws." Some forty different states have some forty different kinds of so-called Blue Sky Laws. Very few of them are any good.

They made it a little more difficult for the legitimate dealer to do business and have not stopped the crook. What we need in this country are criminal acts against the fraudulent selling of securities, or the selling of fraudulent securities by crooked dealers.—JOHN W. PRENTISS.

THE security charlatan lives in a world of unreality.

His conceptions are pure ideas, unblended with facts. The faker is himself frequently his most gullible victim. His imagination dominates him, and at last he comes to believe the story of projected successes of which he glibly tells.

The charlatan becomes a social problem only when he goes to others to finance his dreams and aspirations. The immorality of his conduct is magnified by the fact that the necessities of the case compel him to focus on inexperienced individuals, untutored in the ways of business and finance. A skilled business man, informed about the hazards of investment, is prone to ask disturbing questions, to inquire for tell-tale financial statements, and to permit general skepticism to emanate from him.

And so the faker and his ilk go among the financially illiterate, largely among the folk with only $100 to $1,000 to invest. Though politically prejudiced against malefactors of great wealth among the capitalist classes who exact colossal tolls from industry, frequently these exploited individuals, when confronting the stock salesmen, are secretly hoping to get in on this very swag.

The state of poverty—or even the somewhat higher status of just making ends meet—is, of course, not an ideal state of living. It entails rigorous self-denial, and also the even more difficult negation of desires of dependents for the beautiful commodities of life. In each normal heart springs the hope that perhaps somewhere sometime a magic formula for creating wealth will be discovered. Secretly each ordinary individual is eternally on the lookout for some swifter vehicle to fortune than prosaic hard work and thrift.

How to Detect a Security Charlatan

Perhaps the promoter and his staff who sell engraved certificates of stock and hot air do not understand the subtleties of investment finance, but they do know human nature. They create a product for which there is always a market. Their offerings satisfy these primitive longings for an escape from the drabness of ordinary life. They hold out the prospect of enormous profits. They produce the key to wealth, and let the fancy of the prospective buyer weave the imaginative details around the bare story of certain gains which they relate.

Thus the cure for the fraudulent security evil, which official government estimates indicate takes between $500,000,000 and $1,000,000,000 from the American people annually, lies not wholly in legislation.

Laws may prescribe penalties for material misstatements of facts, but no decrees of legislatures can outlaw the power of suggestion.

The remedy will be found not merely by changing the methods of conscienceless venders, but also in altering the mental processes of the buyer.

In any complete sense, the problem is no doubt insoluble. As long as the institution of private property exists, there will probably be bid and asked quotations for gold bricks.

But the evil can be mitigated by teaching the

masses something of the anatomy and physiology of investments. Such education may influence popular thinking about finance, but, as long as people are what they are, it will not necessarily wholly change feeling and emotions which play a significant rôle in luring folk away from the highway to security.

Security charlatans differ among themselves in degree. In their absolute form, there are those who distribute shares of stock, representing unadulterated hopes and ambitions, unbacked by any tangible intentions to develop physical plants or other assets of a wealth creating character for the benefit of the stockholders. They are selling "blue sky," an ethereal concept whose sole utility is to bring funds to the promoter in exchange for stirring hopes in the investor which will never be fulfilled.

Even more dangerous are the fakers who sell shares in a tangible property, about which significant misrepresentations are made. Such creators of false impressions may have valuable business connections, and may be able with great self-assurance to refer skeptics to banking references. In a strict sense, any broker who places a security in a materially false light is a faker, and the austere investor should be eternally vigilant.

The crude stock salesman, who goes from door to door in quest of dollars from the unsuspecting, be-

[130]

longs to a definite animal species, and, although sub-ject to individual variation, usually bears the common traits.

What are they, and how may the layman recognize them?

A description of the typical charlatan will answer these queries.

To the charlatan, life is simple. The average returns on wishing are exceedingly high. An idea leads on to fortune. Humdrum details, which determine the mortality rate among business enterprises, mean nothing to him. Statistics of overhead costs, competition, probable demand, the purchasing power of consumers—all these blueprints upon which bona fide business success is written never arrest his attention and cause him to pause.

He is ostensibly dealing with a new thought or process, untested in the laboratory of the nation's market places. Accordingly, he must suppress every normal impulse of the buyer to ask for a balance sheet, showing assets and liabilities, or an income account, in which unemotional accountants record the story of success or failure of a business concern. He must keep the eyes of his prospect veered on the future, which is to a large extent unknowable.

The faker forecasts future earnings in consummate detail. He conceals ignorance in a complex of assumptions. He starts with one arbitrary guess, and reasons logically from that premise step by step. But, since his first assumption is probably wrong, his conclusions bear no relation to what actually develops in the careers of such ill guided corporations, whose inner natures are at length revealed in the bankruptcy courts.

Having no tangible records of success, the faker argues by analogy, reciting the facts about the triumphs of the most eminent corporations in the country in allied fields.[1]

Like all fortune tellers, moreover, the security charlatan deals in generalities.

He denounces legitimate bankers, financial editors of reputable newspapers, and others to whom the public may properly turn for unbiased advice. He diverts suspicion from himself by attacking Wall Street and the interests.

Intending to deceive, he misuses the noblest impulses in a free people.

The faker speaks vaguely about profits that will accrue to shareholders from a rise in the value of the shares. An acid test of his sincerity would be to inquire whether there will be a free and open market for the shares, where they can readily be converted into cash. Ordinarily, promotion stocks

[1] For fuller discussion, see Chap. XXII.

are unmarketable, and, even if meritorious, should be purchased only by individuals who are certain not to need their money back for a good many years. Promoters will talk disparagingly of curbstone brokers, on the borderline of financial respectability, who make a market for unlisted shares of companies that represent nothing more than hopes and promises, and, though these middlemen need careful watching, the fact remains that their bids and offers usually constitute the only available means of escape from a financial blunder. "Gyps" they may be, as the promoters say, but legitimate brokers are not interested in securities that seem destined to become worthless.

The itinerant stock salesman, borrowed from the ranks of unemployed plumbers, bookkeepers, incompetent clerks, and other human flotsam and jetsam, gives an automatic sales talk, learned by rote, which is in no sense based on his own analysis or understanding. The shrewd prospect can demonstrate this by asking questions about the physical location of the properties, some of the customers of the concern being financed, accounting details, or any other features which the salesman seems to neglect.

The essence of his method is speed. *He cannot afford to encourage genuine investigation.* To off-

[133]

set it he intimates that the extraordinary opportunities of to-day will not be available to-morrow. Sometimes, he asserts that the supply of stock will be soon exhausted. At other times, he remarks that the selling price will subsequently be raised.

Extraordinary bargains are never—or, to borrow Gilbert's phrase in "Pinafore," well, hardly ever—peddled by stock salesmen. The shrewd investor can always afford to wait for his second thoughts. Legitimate new security offerings are later available as often as not at lower prices in the open market.

A stranger, especially when he introduces himself over the telephone, as the security faker frequently does, is a curious benefactor from whom to expect an opportunity to get rick quick. Exceptionally fine propositions do not need to be hawked from door to door by peddlers, and the mere process of selling securities in this way, consuming 25 to 75 per cent of the funds raised, places an almost insuperable burden on new enterprises, which leads to the presumption of failure, rather than of success.

Questionable promoters deal in names which are symbols of prestige and reliability in communities which they canvass. For example, an operator in Minneapolis promoted the Ford Tractor Company in 1916. In order to get a name for his company, he evidently looked through the local telephone directory until he discovered that there was an electrician by the name of Paul Ford. Getting in touch with him, he made him president and general manager of the tractor company to which he gave the name Ford, then placed full page newspaper advertisements in various cities, trading on the alluring name Ford. In his effort to sell stock to the small investor the promoter asserted that he had built a number of tractors which he had actually never produced and displayed in his literature fake photographs showing a large number of machines and a factory building whose size he materially exaggerated.

He referred to the electrician Ford in his inspirational advertising as a "master builder." The promoter was indicted by a Federal Grand Jury in New York in 1917 on a charge of using the mails to defraud, but he has never come to trial.

Dr. Frederick A. Cook, who discovered the North Pole—or thought he did—recently loomed up as a spectacular figure in the promotion of oil companies. He was the outstanding leader in the development of the "merger" scheme which actually does not merge all the companies which it purports to absorb, but is primarily a device for reloading the shareholders of one defunct company with shares in a new venture in an exchange which involves a cash consideration and probably the purchase of additional shares in the new enterprise.

As trustee of the Petroleum Producers Association, the eminent explorer, according to the investigations of the National Vigilance Committee of the Associated Advertising Clubs of the World, brought about the merger, or attempted consolidation of more than 100 different companies. Dr. Cook at the end of 1923 was tried and sentenced to Federal prison for fourteen years on the charge of using the mails to defraud.

Promoters of an unscrupulous character frequently capitalize the impulse of citizens of small communities to boom their towns at almost any cost. Appealing to the ambitions of local townsmen and pretending that they are going to bring a large new industry to the city, the promoter can frequently count on the gullibility of the local chamber of commerce, local bankers and business men to support schemes which on close analysis prove to be nefarious.

For example, in the spring of 1917 a promoter introduced himself in the town of St. Cloud, Minn., with a barbecue at which he served food and entertainment for more than five thousand individuals. He undertook to sell stock in an automobile company and actually erected a large factory building in this town, bought materials and installed equipment for manufacturing. Perhaps $2,000,000 of the stockholders' money went into these operations. However, his advertising literature was misleading, and he actually produced few cars. He showed a photograph of an automobile which the Government proved had never existed, and gave specifications of a car which he said was to be sold at $1,000 which experts testified could not by any means be built and marketed for the price. He was sentenced in 1923, after losing an appeal, to spend ten years in the Atlanta Penitentiary.

An interesting phase of this case was that the Government indicted twelve leading citizens of St. Cloud along with the prime mover of this enterprise. These citizens had been serving as officers and directors of the company. They were all acquitted, but the fact remains that through the Chamber of Commerce, which had arranged for the promoter to make his headquarters at St. Cloud, which is a city of 12,-000, almost the entire community was lined up solidly behind this enterprise. Salesmen throughout the country would say to a prospect, "Have your bank telegraph to any bank in St. Cloud and you will get back a favorable report." And this was actually true. Salesmen were able to get many bankers throughout the West actually to assist them in the selling of their stock.

Allied to the question of chicanery is the problem of dealing with those who are neither charlatans in a strict sense of the term nor individuals guilty of statutory fraud. Legally, they are entitled to characterization in respectful terms. But, however skillfully they keep within the boundaries of the statutes, they frequently do violence to sound economic doctrine, and their promotions often prove disastrous to innocent investors who are misled by their fine phrases. Technically guilty of no wrong-doing, these men frequently preach beautiful sentiments and sell bad investments.

For example, a New England promoter of finance companies, the unsuccessful fate of whose financial creations has exceeded even the predictions of his critics, trod heavily on the political predilections of individuals. At this writing, he is under indictment for violation of the criminal law, but thus far has been convicted of no crime, and there is no intention in this chapter to impute fraud or charlatanry. However, the record is plain, and it shows how poignant have been the disappointments of needy individuals who heeded his alluring phrases. He sold stock by capitalizing prejudice against Wall Street.

Before the crash, the promoter in the house organ of his stock selling company which was published

How to Detect a Security Charlatan

"in the interest of financial democracy" wrote in a message to his customers: "Nothing will be spared by me, personally, to guarantee protection to all who are clients of our Company, which was organized to do justice, to right an economic wrong."

An article in the same bulletin went on to explain that "the economic injustice consists in the common practice of the using of the moneys of people—who have obtained such moneys over and above their needs for daily living by thrift and self-denial on their part—to make a greater world progress, without returning to these earners and savers of such moneys a true, fair return for the use of their saved capital.

". . . The company hopes to drive out of the field 'wild cat' stock schemes. The company knows that there are in the field to-day, first, the safe, big-yielding investments, and second, the speculative, 'wild cat' stock promotions. It realizes that a man of small means seldom has a chance at the first type and that he is being approached day after day by members of the stock-jobbing fraternity representing the latter type.

The tendency toward alleged altruism often goes to the extreme of assertions by the stock salesmen that the company really does not need the money acutely, but is selling shares for the purpose of

[139]

getting a great community of partners, who will be boosters for the company's product.

As a gesture, they announce that no individual may buy more than one, five, or ten shares as the case may be.

For example, an Arizona copper company, whose operations were recently stopped by an injunction of the Attorney General of New York, purported to decline to sell to any individual more than $100 of its stock of $.50 par value.

The overzealous sales representative of a legit-imate financial house may reveal one or two of the symptoms of the purveyor of fraud, but no reputable vender will display all or even a major part of the symptoms of the faker. The more subtle charla-tans, knowing the conventional methods, seek con-sciously to avoid revealing the common traits, and is more difficult for the layman to spot.

CHAPTER XIV

BUCKET SHOPS—AND HOW TO KEEP OUT OF THEM

Exposure of the Lures of the Great Pretenders who lurk in the Shadow of Wall Street

The new bucket shop is a more sinister affair than the old, not only because it steals the people's money as it was stolen in the old days, but because, in most cases, it has an underground backing of tremendous influence and weight, because it is supported by men whose position in the community has the appearance of being free from any taint or connection with such vicious operations.—SEYMOUR L. CROMWELL.

BUCKET shops are another device which man has invented to frustrate the will of man.

Guided by a simple hope and tugged by wild desires, folks stream endlessly into those strange bazaars of finance which trade on popular delusions. Bucketeers, who falsely represent themselves as brokers, extract their profit out of the science of deceit and by means of their expert knowledge of human frailties.

A bucket shop has the outward physical setting of a brokerage office where securities are bought and sold. But a bucket shop has the appearance without the reality. A man who trades through a bucket shop is ineffective because his agent fails to do what he is intended to do. The customer is expressing his attitude regarding prospective changes in the market worth of securities, expecting to profit out of rises and falls in quotations, but, if he trades through a bucket shop instead of in a respectable brokerage office, he watches the fluctuating prices in vain. He is as futile as a blindfolded man touching the keys of a typewriter and failing to make an impression on paper because by some tampering with the machinery the type bars have been disconnected from the keys.

The communications of the customer of a bucket shop with the great market places where prices of securities and commodities are quoted have been cut off by subtle tinkering with the machinery of brokerage.

He gets all the thrills and excitement of one actually operating in the stock and commodity markets, but he interests himself in vain in the trend of quotations, for the bucketeer has seen to it that, in all probability, the customer will lose no matter how unconventionally and perversely prices may move.

Bucket Shops

A bucket shop—and in its present loose usage the term covers the whole range of irregularities evolved by the consciously unethical brokers who are bent on preventing their customers from winning—is a center of delusions.

The purchaser of securities assumes wrongly that the keeper of the bucket shop is his agent, ready to buy stocks, bonds or commodities at regular exchanges for a commission. Where the customer buys out of proportion to his means he has to borrow to hold his commitments. By an arrangement with the banks, the reputable broker gets the needed funds by pledging the securities as collateral and the customer must pay interest on the borrowed money as long as the loan is carried. The broker pays the interest charges to the bank, and in turn collects interest from his customers, usually adding a small profit to reimburse him for his trouble. The ordinary commission broker, who acts as an agent in the purchase or sale of securities for outsiders, whom Wall Street conveniently calls the public, makes money out of the transactions only in two ways: through the charge of a commission and through a profit made on interest.

The margin of profit is small and success depends on a large volume of business. The legitimate broker neither profits nor loses from the correctness of judgment of his customer. He prefers to have customers of discernment, for all others are quickly wiped out and effaced when they enter the necessarily hazardous and baffling task of seeking gains out of their own judgment of the future worth of securities or commodities. Experience shows that the great leaps of speculation are only for those especially qualified with knowledge and financial resources. The ordinary man, whose notions about the financial machinery are vague and whose knowledge of the forces that determine market values is hazy, sooner or later is likely to lose the funds which he has offered as a sacrifice at the great temples of speculation to the god of Avarice.

Bucketing, ancient and modern, is based on the discovery that the average man's judgment of the future trend of market prices is likely to be wrong, and the bucketeer, unlike the reputable broker, makes all that his customers lose. And, since bucketeers are faithless violators of the statutory laws and of the ordinary principles of decency, they secretly and cunningly gear up their machinery to heighten the probabilities of loss to the customer. They have nothing to gain if the customer persistently profits and everything to gain if he loses.

Illicit trade relations probably started shortly after Eve succeeded in putting across a sales talk about

Bucket Shops

apples to Adam. Although there is no evidence or likelihood that Eve was mercenary and acting as the representative of a coöperative association of apple growers, it is probable that soon after the time of Creation a minority of traders sacrificed ethics for profit. The remarkable fact about the present world of finance and business is not that bad practices persist, but that we have reached a stage where business and money lending have so heightened their prestige that they can talk unblushingly of business morality. In finance the bucketeer and the swindler hurt the honest broker and reputable bond houses because they tend to weaken public confidence in the whole financial machinery of the country.

Bucketing is an American institution and, like the pork barrel, one of the few of which patriots cannot be proud. The practice is a reflex of the ticker system, by which prices quoted at the principal exchanges are instantly revealed throughout the nation. Bucket shops deal in quotations, rather than in commodities and securities, and their birth came shortly after the Chicago Board of Trade began publicly to disseminate its quotations some fifty years ago. Soon after, the New York Stock Exchange developed a system for giving free and open publicity to the prices at which all transactions on the floor are made.

In its pure form, the original bucket-shop was a

frank betting place, where the keeper matched his judgment of future prices against that of his customers. The system was applied to grain, cotton and securities.

The name bucket shop crept into the language without formal baptism and its true origin is still in dispute. Some energetic candidate for the degree of doctor of philosophy might well delve into the subject to dissipate doubts and to still controversy. Perhaps the most widely-held version is that the name as well as the system was invented in Chicago, which H. G. Wells once called "that singular relapse into barbarism."

When the Chicago Board of Trade years ago forbade dealings in "options" of less than 5,000 bushels, the "Open Board of Trade" was established to meet the needs of small gamblers bent on operating, despite the attempt to cut them off. The open board brokers functioned below the rooms of the Board of Trade and, according to traditions, when business on the Board of Trade was slack, the elevator used by members would be sent down to bring up from the open board what was known as a "bucketful" of the smaller speculators. It has been suggested that this expression was borrowed from the terminology of mining, for miners go up and down the shafts in ore buckets.

Bucket Shops

Another version, according to which the term has been imported, traces the word to the habits of a gang of rowdies in the East End of London who used to drain the empty ale and rum kegs which they came upon in the street and then retire to their meeting place and hold a celebration with their dregs. These gangs came to be known as "bucketers" or "bucket shoppers," and because of their illicit conduct the term was gradually extended to other disreputable groups. And students of bucket shops are confronted with the suggestion that the British name for those who drained kegs was by analogy applied to Americans who instead drained purses.

In its pristine days the bucket shop was unpretentious. It made its headquarters in out of the way places, at the back doorsteps of the great market places. New Street was cluttered with the old-fashioned bucket shops when they flourished in New York. The offices were furnished simply—often with merely a desk, a telephone and a ticker. By their appearance they automatically told the patron what they were, and there was relatively little confusion about them. For the most part customers went to them for the conscious purpose of betting as to whether prices would rise or fall. They were dirty, unattractive gambling places for office boys, clerks, racetrack touts and a whole miscellany of humanity who had red-hot tips on the market but lacked the financial means of speculating. The bucket shop would accept accounts on one-point margin, whereas the legitimate broker required at least 10 per cent. Bucket shops made speculation easy and cheap for those least able to afford the luxury. Clerks of Stock Exchange firms and banks, who are not permitted to speculate, often were tempted to evade the rules by operating through bucket shops. In the financial underworld bucket shop keepers have long capitalized the fears of customers who were afraid to have it known they were trading, and hence perpetually lacked the courage to bring action against those guilty of the most irregular and dishonest of practices.

The old-fashioned bucket shop has waned, and has tended to become obsolete.

The crude, elementary bucket shop, which obviously violates state laws designed to check it, has been supplanted by a subtler organization, which operates differently but achieves the same purpose of enabling the keeper to make all his customers lose. Present day scientific bucket shops actually buy and sell stocks for their customers and pretend in every way to be legitimate brokers. Physically, their appearance suggests elegance and great resources. Through experience the unfortunate customers have learned that there is no correlation between the exquisite character of the rugs and mahogany furniture and the ethics of the broker. Modern bucket shops are luxuriously fitted offices not situated on the doorsteps of Wall Street, but on the main highways of finance. Recently, as New York has moved up town, a New Wall Street has grown up in the shopping district around Forty-second Street, and, whereas some of the most reputable houses have opened branches in that district, scores of questionable brokers have gone up town to get the new trade.

In the new style bucket shop orders to buy stock, for example, are executed. The bucketeer purchases the securities from a firm which is a member of a stock exchange, and is able to show his customers a confirmation of the purchase. This stroke is designed to help comply with the law and to give material to answer the doubts of customers.

But instead of holding the stock for the customers the questionable broker either immediately or within a few days resells it, thus avoiding the expense of holding it, which involves interest charges. Let's assume that the customer has purchased ten shares of Atchison, Topeka & Santa Fe Railroad through a bucket shop and that the market worth was exactly $1,000. In this hypothetical case the customer puts up $100 as margin, and the other $900 is presumably financed by the broker who borrows at the bank. In brokerage parlance the customer has a debit balance of $900 on which he has to pay interest. The bucket shop, which buys the stock and then sells it out, gives the customer the impression that he is holding the shares for him, and each month charges him interest on the fictitious debit balance. The interest payments are pure profit for the bucketeer, who has also appropriated the $100 margin, instead of keeping it as a buffer to represent the customer's equity in the shares and a safety cushion to take care of any decline in the market.

According to brokerage practice, the customer's margin is the first to suffer losses in case of an adverse movement of quotations in the market. If Atchison, purchased at 100, declines to 90, the customer's margin is effaced, and he is confronted with the choice of putting up additional funds as a new margin or of relinquishing the shares, ordering the broker to sell them and of consequently losing the original margin. The bucketeer calls for more margin, even as the legitimate broker does, but he in effect appropriates the new margin unto himself. In accepting interest payments on a debit balance the bucketeer is guilty of grand larceny and subjects himself to the possibility of a jail sentence extending ten years. This whole machinery for failing to re-

Bucket Shops

tain securities that bucketeers pretend to carry involves violations of the New York State law, and invites conviction under laws relating to bucketing, taking a position opposite customers' intentionally improper hypothecation of securities, and conversion.

There is an ebb and flow of periods of indignation against the bucket shops. Since bucketeers gain what their customers lose, they thrive during periods of declining security prices, such as the country passed through between the fall of 1919 and August, 1921, because the average customer buys securities on the assumption that prices will rise. In time of upward surging quotations, bucket shops are beset with difficulties, and are often forced to discontinue rather than pay out profits to successful customers. And since it is common for bucketeers to operate under assumed names, they close down one establishment that has guessed the market trend incorrectly and start another under a new name.

The evils that the bucketeers do would be serious if they merely swindled those who want to take high fliers in the stock market, but they become an active, social menace when they hoodwink those intending, not to speculate, but to purchase high grade investment bonds. And in recent revelations there has been ample proof that the investor as well as the speculator has suffered. Questionable houses have

[151]

exploited the partial payment plan, urging customers to purchase more securities than they could hope to pay for, on the assumption that after a few payments were made the customer would become discouraged, stop payments and lose what had been paid in. And in the cases where purchasers completed their payments, they would often find that the so-called broker did not have the securities on hand to deliver.

Where the bucketeers were caught without a supbly of securities previously purchased they would ingeniously invent seemingly plausible excuses. Some of the shops kept 15 per cent of the amount of the securities required, and would use them over and again to show to different customers to assure them that the stocks and bonds were on hand. Sometimes the bucketeer would borrow securities to show to his skeptical customers.

The irregularities in such cases are often technical, becoming evident only to one who can intelligently read the books. Where a bucketeer purchased securities and then resold them, the selling would frequently be done through a dummy account in the name of a real person who was well paid for the use of his cognomen. Sometimes the bucketeer would run two separate offices under different names, and would buy through one and sell through the other for the purpose of appearing to carry out the order of his customers and yet avoid the expense of retaining securities. Another device was to control a finance company, borrow from the subsidiary through loans secured by stocks, which the finance company would promptly sell.

The bucketeer simulates the real broker, and the layman often has difficulty in detecting the former. The faker frequently operates over the telephone, calling up strangers to inform them of easy opportunities to attain quickly, the wealth of a Crœsus. The bucketeer employs "business getters" to attract "suckers" to the office and pays them commissions far in excess of the commission given the broker by his customer. The questionable broker often offers reduced rates for executing orders and agrees to keep down interest charges on a debit balance. Where he makes impossible concessions he protects himself either by bucketing or by incorrectly reporting the purchase or sale price to the customer.

Illicit brokerage thrives partly as a result of the imperfection in the legitimate financial machinery and partly as a result of the greed of the public. The salvation lies in making the whole business of finance conform more precisely to the requirements of society and also in education. For the ordinary mortal, speculation, even when executed by honest brokers, is usually a profitless adventure, whereas sound investment is a reasonably sure road to the accumulation of the means of staying out of the poor-house toward the end of an active life. Speculation involves unusual risk in the hope of making a huge profit. Investment, on the other hand, looks forward only to regular income and safety of principal.

CHAPTER XV

HIGH FINANCE—AND THE PUBLIC GOOD

Services of Investment Brokers and Stock Exchanges; How Wall Street Does its Day's Work.

It is unquestionable that only a small part of the transactions upon the Exchange is of an investment character; a substantial part may be characterized as virtually gambling. Yet we are unable to see how the state could distinguish between proper and improper transactions by law since the forms and mechanisms are identical.—REPORT OF HUGHES COMMISSION OF 1909.

Importance must be attached to the protection and safeguards which organized stock exchanges give the stock and bond holder, in regulating brokerage transactions and maintaining a standard of commercial honor among brokers. The value of this organization becomes apparent when we take account of the gigantic frauds perpetrated upon innocent investors through advertising campaigns by persons unaffiliated with any recognized Exchange.—S. S. HUEBNER.

The stock market acts as a reservoir and distributor of capital, with something of the same efficiency with which

[155]

a series of well-regulated locks and dams operate to equalize the irregular current of a river.—CHARLES A. CONANT.

What amazing misconceptions and popular prejudices are interwoven in the concepts "High Finance," and Wall Street! In certain of the provinces politicians regularly support themselves and elect their candidates by denouncing the narrow street that runs from Trinity Church to the East River. Moreover, subtle promoters who create whatever popular fancy and prejudice demand, sell questionable securities in abundance by denouncing the financial autocracy of Wall Street and characterizing their enterprise as the forerunner of democracy in finance. A New England promoter who was less helpful to his security customers than he promised to be, waxed eloquent some years ago about democracy in finance. Democracy in finance constitutes an alluring phrase, but beware of the stock jobber who seeks to cash in on it!

Wall Street is perhaps no more virtuous nor worse than the counting room of the ordinary commercial enterprise. Wall Street is the cash drawer of the nation's business.

The job of investment bankers is to gather from all parts of the land rivulets of investment funds and lead them into a great central stream of capital, from

[156]

which the massive corporate enterprises of the country can draw funds for their development. The bankers of Wall Street are essentially middlemen, bringing borrowers and lenders together.

High grade investment bankers are more than mere brokers. They buy the securities from the borrower themselves and run the risk of not being able to resell them to the investing public. Part of their underwriting fee is the payment for the assumption of that hazard.

Moreover, investment bankers assume a moral responsibility for the genuineness and investment value of their offerings. Perhaps there is not a house whose judgment has not occasionally erred—to write in euphemistic terms—but in case of trouble, the investment banker forms protective committees and endeavors to salvage the interest of those to whom they sold bonds.

Moreover, even before financial storms, investment bankers frequently sit in on boards of directors of companies that they finance and make sure that borrowed funds are administered in accordance with standards which they consider sound. Sometimes bankers go further than exercising this negative power of veto. They occasionally dominate enterprises which they finance and turn the business executives into super-clerks who do little more than

[157]

carry out the will of the bankers. Such interference frequently robs an enterprise of the originality and peculiar individuality which come from the expression of the real personality of its founders and managers. It has frequently tended to drive enterprises to the rocks, particularly when such control is associated with inefficient financing entailing the creation of more securities than the actual tangible property behind the enterprise and its earning power warrant.

Bankers are human beings and are no less subject to error than their fellow men in other vocations. However, when the investment banker adheres to the standards of his own profession and provides solid enterprise with funds that are genuinely needed in restricted amounts on economical terms, he is facilitating the production and distribution of goods and quickening the tempo of economic life.

Moreover, he is at the same time forging securities worthy of the thrift funds of investors.

When, however, instead of being satisfied with the margins of legitimate commissions he controls enterprises for the purpose of milking them and for surrounding them with capital structures far in excess of their real needs, he is creating watered securities which eventually are almost certain to result in loss for those who acted on his advice.

The broker who does not create securities, but who

merely buys and sells outstanding issues as an agent for his customers also plays a necessary rôle in the present financial scheme. He not only brings buyers and sellers of securities together, but he assures his customer that he will give him the benefit of bids and offers on securities in which he is interested from all parts of the world.

The stock exchange is a market place. It is a common meeting ground for buyers and sellers of securities from all parts of the world. Organized markets give securities which are listed for trading on them an important additional attribute—ready marketability, or liquidity—the capacity of being turned into cash in ordinary circumstances on a moment's notice.

If it were not for the presence of highly developed organized markets, investment would be a far more permanent matter. One could only put funds into enterprises which could be left undisturbed indefinitely.

For services rendered the charges of stock and bond brokers are moderate. The usual commission is a little more than $\frac{1}{8}$ of 1 per cent of the par value of the securities bought or sold for a customer. In the case of new creation of securities, no commission over and above the offering price is charged.

Having selected a broker, the bond buyer meets

with little difficulty in executing an order. He may either visit the office of the bond house and see a salesman there or may be called upon by a representative of the house at his office or home, or may give the instructions over the telephone. The following morning he receives in the mail a confirmation of the order which reveals the cost of the bonds and the amount of commission. The rate of commission on bonds is $1.50 per $1,000 face value of bonds, with a customary minimum charge of $1 to $2. The buyer must remit on the same day he receives the bill, or interest will be charged for the period that elapses until the debt is discharged.

Buying or selling of stocks is carried on in the same manner. The unit of trade on the New York Stock Exchange is 100 shares. Any block less than 100 shares is referred to as an odd lot and may be purchased through any member house, but the price on the odd lot is $\frac{1}{8}$ to $\frac{1}{4}$ of a point less favorable than that on a hundred share unit. In reporting a transaction to a customer the broker must reveal the name of the broker to whom he has sold the stock or from whom he has bought it.

New York Stock Exchange brokers charge a minimum of $7.50 for buying or selling 100 shares of stock selling at less than $10 a share. The commission is $15 a hundred shares for stock selling between $10 and $125. The minimum is $20 a hundred shares for stock selling higher than $125 a share. Commissions for odd lots are in proportion, subject to the usual minimum charges of $1 to $2.

Where full payment is not made by the customer, the transaction becomes a margin account, and physical control of the stocks remains with the broker until the customer has paid for them in full or sold them. The margin is the sum which the customer puts up with the broker as his equity in the transaction. The broker himself must insist that customers keep their margin intact, irrespective of changes in the market price of the securities.

If a customer buys United States Steel common at $100 a share and puts up a margin of 20 per cent, his equity would be effaced if the stock declined to 80. In that event the broker would notify his customer to put up more funds (or additional margin) and if he failed to do so, the broker would sell out the steel stock at the market price to protect himself from loss. In such circumstances the customer would lose his equity in the transaction.

In such dealings the broker must supply the other 80 per cent of the cost of the stock. He does this partly by drawing on his own capital but chiefly by using the securities themselves as collateral for a loan from the banks on which interest must be paid.

The broker passes on the interest charges to his customer and adds something to the charges to compensate him for his activity.

The commodity exchanges such as the New York Cotton Exchange and the Chicago Board of Trade (the wheat pit) serve a slightly different function. They create the machinery by which speculators in commodities can discount or anticipate the future. Through hedging, the commodity exchange makes it possible for cotton goods houses and flour millers, for example, to eliminate the risks of changes in the price of raw materials. The cotton converter sometimes buys his raw cotton months in advance of selling his finished cotton goods. The price of the latter will depend upon the quotation for raw cotton prevailing at the time he is offering the cotton goods for sale. When he is actually buying the raw cotton he does not know what the price of the commodity will be some weeks hence. He therefore hedges, selling for future delivery an amount of cotton equivalent to that which he is buying at the present time. Thus, if the price of raw cotton rises, his actual cotton will appreciate with the market, whereas he will lose an equivalent sum in later buying additional cotton to satisfy his contract to deliver the commodity at a future time. If, on the other hand, cotton prices decline, his cotton on hand will depreciate. How-

[162]

ever, he will be able to buy cotton to deliver against his future contract at a lower price than that at which the agreement was made. Hedging is a device for offsetting losses with gains so that the merchant can figure in advance precisely what the cost of his raw material will be.

The number of individuals who trade in the basic commodities is very small compared to those who invest or speculate in stocks and bonds, but the practice of farmers and others directly involved in the production of these commodities of using the great commodity exchanges as places to sell out in advance, in case they believe prices will decline, is increasing.

Trading in cotton for future delivery on the New York Cotton Exchange is in contracts of 100 bales of 500 pounds each. Quotations on cotton as reported in the daily press are in cents and hundredths of a cent a pound. The minimum fluctuations, therefore, represent a variation of $5 in the value of each contract of 100 bales. The commission charge is $12.50 for the sale or purchase of one contract when the price is 25 cents a pound or less, the commission is $15.00 a contract when the price is from 25.01 to 30 cents a pound, and from 31.01 to 35 cents a pound the commission is $17.50 a contract.

In grains the Chicago Board of Trade furnishes the primary world market. Contracts there are in units of 5000 bushels or multiples thereof. The typical contract is for 10,000 bushels. Quotations, as carried in the newspapers, are in cents a bushel. The brokerage commission is $12.50 for a round trade of the sale and purchase of 5000 bushels.

Coffee and sugar are traded in on the New York Coffee and Sugar Exchange. A contract of coffee is 250 bags or 3,250 pounds, and the minimum fluctuation is $\frac{1}{100}$ of a cent. Commissions are $12.50 a contract bought or sold when the price is below 10 cents and $15 when it is between 10 cents and 19.99 cents. Raw sugar is traded in contracts of 50 tons of 2240 pounds. The minimum fluctuations are the same as in coffee, and the commission charges are $12.50 a contract when the price is below 4 cents, $15 when the price is between 4 cents and 9.99 cents and higher when the price is 10 cents or more.

Commodity trading is carried on to a large extent on a marginal basis. Conservative houses require a margin of $700 a contract in cotton. In grains the margin is usually $300 for 5000 pounds of wheat, $200 on corn and $150 on oats. In times of financial stress usually the requirements are more stringent.

CHAPTER XVI

HAS THE DAY OF OPPORTUNITIES PASSED?

A Study of New Frontiers and the Disappearance of Free Land.

. . . Since the days when the fleet of Columbus sailed into the waters of the New World, America has been another name for opportunity, and the people of the United States have taken their tone from the incessant expansion which has not only been open but has been forced upon them.

He would be a rash prophet who would assert that the expansive character of American Life has now entirely ceased. Movement has been its dominant fact, and, unless this training has no effect upon a people, the American energy will continually demand a wider field for its exercise.

But never again will such gifts of free land offer themselves. For a moment, at the frontier, the bonds of custom are broken and unrestraint is triumphant. There is no *tabula rasa*, the stubborn American environment is there with its imperious summons to accept its conditions; the inherent ways of doing things are also there; and yet, in spite of environment, and in spite of custom, each frontier

[165]

did indeed furnish a new field of opportunity, a gate of escape from the bondage of their past, and freshness and confidence, and scorn of older society, impatient of its restraints and ideas, and indifferent to its lessons, have accompanied the frontier.

What the Mediterranean sea was to the Greeks, breaking the bond of custom, offering new experiences, calling out new institutions and activities, that, and more, the ever re-treating frontier has been to the United States directly, and to the nations of Europe more remotely.

And now, four centuries from the discovery of America, at the end of a hundred years of life under the Constitution, the frontier has gone, and with its going has closed the first period of American history.—FREDERICK JACKSON TURNER.

Psychologists characterize the universal yearn-ing for the good old days as the obliviscence of the unpleasant. The human mind has a tendency to forget the hardships and the bitterness of bygone days and to remember only the more pleasant as-pects. Pessimists in each new generation look back into the pages of history and sigh bitterly be-cause the day of opportunities to do things has passed forever.

From the time of its accidental discovery by Co-lumbus in 1492 up to 1890 when the last of the free land in the United States was exhausted, America was looked upon as the land of opportunity. Work-ers in the city, if oppressed, had the alternative of going west and settling on land which they could acquire for the asking. Even serious-minded economists wondered at the beginning of the last decade of the 19th century whether the day of extraordinary opportunities in the United States had passed with the exhaustion of areas of free land. With all the choicest agricultural area privately owned, it was feared that America would become like the Old World, a place of slow and gradual plodding rather than what it had historically been, a hunting ground for pathfinders and pioneers, a place where miraculous and colossal growth had become a commonplace development. But strangely enough, with the disappearance of free land other economic forces came into play which more than offset the seemingly adverse development. The growth of the country since 1890 has been wholly out of proportion with the slow pace before that year when free land was still available.

The national income has grown as follows:

[1] 1890	12 billion dollars
1900	18 billion dollars
1910	32 billion dollars
1920	60 billion dollars [1]

The buying power of the population was never greater than in 1923 and 1924. The average per capita income in dollars, which of course varies in purchasing power through the business cycles, has shown a tendency to move steadily upward in the United States, as indicated by the following table:

Date	Per capita income
[1] 1850	$ 95
1870	174
1890	192
1900	332
1918	586 [1]

By the introduction of efficient methods in agriculture, more produce has been raised per capita despite the disappearance of free land. The following table shows productions per capita illustrating this point:

	1900	1920	
[1] Wheat	54.9	78.1	(bushels)
Corn	205.4	301.	(bushels)
Cotton	.0976	.1247	(bales)
Rice	24.5	135.5	(pounds)
Sugar Beets	16	135.3	(pounds) [1]

Moreover during this period there has been in the United States a tremendous development of the theory of mass production through the increased use of automatic repetitive machinery. This revolution

[1] From Julius H. Barnes's "The Genius of American Business."

in industrial technique has made business leaders strive perpetually to widen the market for commodities through cheapening the price. The classic example of this method is that used by Henry Ford in the sale of cheap automobiles and tractors.

The development of big business during the 20th century has changed the habits and ambitions of the younger generation which looks increasingly to profitable employment by large corporations rather than ownership of small independent enterprises. The multiplication of large economic units whose operations extend throughout the continent has enormously increased the demand for managerial skill. The number of jobs with emoluments as large as that the President of the United States receives is greater than ever before.

The development of the machinery of the money markets and other channels of investment reaching into every city and town in the country forms the background which facilitates the launching and development of colossal enterprises designed to serve efficiently and economically genuine human needs.

Apart from the opportunities of the cities, great sections of the country in the West and Southweast and parts of the South are still thinly populated and offer fertile fields for development.

[169]

CHAPTER XVII

A FORMULA FOR EFFECTIVE THRIFT

Avoidable and Accidental Factors which Frustrate those who Would be Prudent.

The best plan of life insurance is the plan that will enable you to buy as much protection as you can afford as quickly as possible.—HENRY BRUÈRE.

IN the ranks of those who die penniless are many who perceived the philosophic merits of thrift. Pious hopes of leading an economically sound life have in many instances been frustrated.

Unless an individual sets out more or less consciously to offset the factors that are likely to block his thrift impulses, he may be deterred from development along the lines of economic rationalism.

Internal psychological tendencies and external events alike conspire to drive the individual toward the disastrous paths of thriftlessness and improvidence. The intention to save, to live within a budget, involves an intellectual decision fraught with little emotional content. On the other hand, instinc-

[170]

tive animal impulses tend to militate against the carrying out of the program.

What are the elements conspiring against economic well being?

Greed and avarice

Extravagance

Bad judgment or advice

Gambling tendencies

Faulty investment technique

The foregoing deal with the individual himself—his character and his training. To succeed fully, an individual must gain control of himself and regulate potential, wayward tendencies which exist more or less in all individuals and which, if uncontrolled, lead him astray financially. Before he can obtain economic independence through his own efforts he must first be master of his own soul.

There are, however, factors that sometimes frustrate the thrifty which lie wholly outside the influence of the human will. These include

Accidents,

Illness,

Premature death,

Unemployment.

Nicely balanced, statistically correct programs for building up an investment fund which will lead to independence in twenty years may be ruthlessly upset by a careless taxi driver who suddenly blots the saver out of existence or hopelessly cripples him.

Or a chronic malady may seize hold of an individual and not only interfere with saving but actually use up the accumulated thrift funds.

These contingencies and even unemployment can be anticipated and provided against through insurance which is simply a collective device for transferring hazards from the individual to a group. Though the career of an individual is unpredictable, that of the group can be forecast with minute precision.

Life insurance makes the human will effective in financial matters. It is a force which translates good intentions into accomplishments.

It constitutes a certain means of creating an asset free from the hazards to which other schemes are subject.

Many foolish men seek to compare the relative advantages of life insurance and bonds. Some argue that good bonds yield more than insurance and that, if they should put their money regularly into sound bonds instead of into the treasury of an insurance company, they would be richer at the end of twenty years. Perhaps they would be if able to select the right kind of securities,—except for one enormous element of risk.

A Formula for Effective Thrift

The man who buys only bonds figures on the investment risk, forgetting the greater hazard in respect to the span of his own life. During the second year of accumulation, for example, a misdirected steering wheel may suddenly terminate the existence of the investor who will perish with scarcely more than 5 per cent of the estate he planned. Accidents may relentlessly nullify the noblest impulses of the individual who aspires to protect the lives of his wife and children through his own savings.

Life insurance, on the other hand, is a means of immediately transforming a wish into an assured fact. If a man decides to take a $20,000 policy and pays his first premium of $500, no factor can prevent the execution of his plan. Death through accidental or natural means will bring the full face value of the policy to his beneficiaries. If he dies soon, then the yield on his investment becomes prodigious—greater by far than the widest promises of the most unscrupulous stock salesman.

Life insurance then must be regarded primarily as protection against the possibility of premature death, which every individual faces. Since everyone dies, every policy in good standing eventually matures. If a man were assured that he would live a stipulated number of years, he might do better with his money than to buy life insurance. But since none has a guarantee clause in his contract with nature, everyone with dependents, present or prospective, ought to give insurance a place in his financial program.

For pure protection, ordinary life is the best policy, for with the exception of term insurance, which has limited uses only, it gives the greatest coverage for the least expenditure. Each individual should have his own needs analyzed by an insurance expert. In general, however, it may be said that ordinary life is virtually always the most suitable form of policy for the man over thirty with dependents.

Younger men, who are asked to pay lower rates, can consider the more luxurious policies such as limited payment (usually twenty payment) life or endowment policies. These forms of insurance are more expensive than straight insurance and give no greater protection in case of death. They combine in varying degrees coverage against the risk of being cut off prematurely with investment features. Twenty payment life and endowment policies have a greater cash surrender value than ordinary life and also a bigger borrowing allowance.

The fancier policies have the merit of compulsory saving. A man can achieve this same objective by buying straight life, and at the same time making a contract with a well conducted building and loan association to save a stipulated sum each month over a period of twelve years. Such a combination will yield more whether the insured lives or dies during the term of the policy.

If a man were certain of dying before twenty years the ordinary life policy would demonstrably be the best, for it would give as much as the others for less money. If a man were sure of living twenty years or more, then there would be something to be said for limited payment and endowment policies. The advantages of the limited payment policies are largely psychological, wholly independ ent of the statistics of the situation.

The ordinary human being derives satisfaction from the knowledge that at a stipulated time in his life his insurance needs will have always been taken care of. The same feeling applies to endowment policies where the rate is higher. At the end of twenty years the individual can either continue his insurance or withdraw his cash allowance from the company. The cash surrender value will be smallest on ordinary life, larger on limited payment, and still larger on endowment policies. At the time the endowment policy matures the cash surrender value coincides exactly with the face amount of the policy.

For the man who lacks the will power to save,

without compulsion or the technical skill for making good investments, endowment policies serve a useful purpose. They yield less than all but the very highest grade of bonds, but endowment policies entail a high degree of safety. The financially illiterate person who buys an endowment policy on which he pays annual premiums has the satisfaction of knowing that canny investment specialists at the headquarters of an insurance company will watch his funds with consummate skill. He has thus freed himself from the danger of buying worthless securities by which he might, like thousands of others, lose his principal.

Twenty payment life is especially suitable for men under thirty who are not hard pressed financially and who can afford something better than the cheapest form of policy. Twenty payment policies are adapted to the tastes of men of this group who believe in their hearts that they are going to live twenty years and are willing to speculate on the fact.

When in doubt, the prospective insured should buy ordinary life, for having once been accepted into a company as physically and morally fit, he can always convert a cheaper policy into a more expensive one. It is best to buy as much insurance as the buyer can afford when he is acceptable to the company. Switches into more costly policies can always be made, if desired, later in life when the insured is likely to be better off financially and worse off physically.

The danger of waiting is that one of an infinite variety of diseases may render one ineligible for insurance. It is one of the real tragedies of life that the physically disqualified clamor for insurance, whereas those eligible for it ordinarily will not partake of the privilege without the most persistent persuasion on the part of an agent.

Of all present day salesmen, few if any, sell a more useful service than the life insurance agent— and yet he is despised more than any other. This anomaly is partly his own fault and in part ascribable to stupidity on the part of the public. Of course, some of the older generation remember the early history of life insurance, when it was frequently a fraud and always unscientific.

Until recently, life insurance selling had not reached the plane of a profession. Failures in other vocations gravitated to insurance and sought to make sales on the basis of seeking favors from relatives and friends rather than through a genuine understanding of the needs of clients.

The new insurance agent renders service in laying out programs and suggesting policies that fit particular requirements. As modern life becomes more complex, new uses are found. The levying of inheritance taxes in recent years has, for example, led to widespread buying of life insurance by wealthy men to provide cash for the payment of death duties.

The policy holder should seek insurance with the same avidity and interest with which he buys cigarettes, baseball tickets, and clothing. He should no longer purchase insurance reluctantly as the best way of getting rid of an agent who has proved a nuisance. If the agent appreciated the dignity of his calling and realized that life insurance is the most difficult of all services and commodities to buy, he would escape from the odium of being bothersome. What other institution shows the independence of an insurance company, which thumps your chest, listens to your heart-beat, asks you impertinent questions about your personal habits and about the behavior of your grandmother before it will accept your patronage?

By taking out an insurance policy the individual removes all the financial uncertainty associated with death. The insurance company, for its part, is taking no chance, for, though an individual's life is uncertain in duration, that of a large group is definitely predictable. The insurance companies operate in accordance with the American Experience

[178]

table, which is based on the records of the past. Periodical health examinations and general medical advance, especially in respect to preventive work, tend to lengthen the average life. As this development continues, life insurance will become cheaper.

Individuals dependent upon their own physical and mental labor for a livelihood face other personal hazards besides death. Their main capital is a sound body and mind, and earning power depends upon their physical well being. Unlike the business man whose enterprise will run on just the same when he is bedridden, the employee is likely to lose his income when he is indisposed.

Unless protected by capital reserves, the ordinary individual cannot afford to assume the risk of sickness or accident. He should transfer this hazard to an insurance company. In buying health and accident insurance he should buy a non-cancellable policy. The cancellation clause in health and accident policies is one of the most deceptive in present day insurance and is evil because many policy holders do not understand its real significance. The cancellation clause gives the company the right to cancel a policy after paying a claim when it believes that the policy holder's health has been impaired and that the same illness or related maladies may recur.

[179]

In applying for a non-cancellable policy such as that written by the Pacific Mutual Co., of California, or the Massachusetts Accident Co., the would-be policy holder must undergo a physical examination, and, if accepted, he remains insured at least up to the age of sixty, provided he pays his annual premiums, irrespective of the future status of his health.

Selecting a company is a specialized matter. When in doubt it is well to consult a banker. Every individual ought to select an insurance agent just as he seeks out a physician or dentist, and be willing to follow his advice.

In general, one should bear in mind that rates are nearly the same in any of the well managed companies and usually one gets what one pays for. The mutual companies, which are owned by the policy holders, are run for service, not profit. They are among the best companies in the country, though not invariably the cheapest.

In taking out accident and health policies an individual ought to buy enough to take care of at least his minimum living requirements in case of disability. In buying life insurance, he should buy enough to create a fund, which, if invested at 5 per cent, would take care of the requirements of his dependents. In estimating his family needs he should deduct his own personal expenditures and savings, and remember too that his family can be expected to economize a little after the bread winner has gone into the great beyond.

However, few need to be warned against buying too much insurance. The average man is under-insured, particularly since the purchasing power of the dollar has shrunken since 1913.

Insurance against unemployment has not gained much headway in this country. In England and continental European countries, the government fosters unemployment insurance. Where the government contributes to the maintenance of the system it is in the nature of doles or charity and somewhat apart from the problems of this volume. In the United States a common form of unemployment insurance is membership in trade unions, many of which have funds to take care of members out of work. The white collar man or professional worker can perhaps best provide against the risk of a break in continuous employment by saving and setting up a definite reserve against such a contingency.

In summary, an effective formula is one that provides for the regular investor a background of insurance which will offset external and unavoidable factors which might otherwise frustrate those who would be thrifty.

[181]

CHAPTER XVIII

SECRETS OF THE FINANCIAL PAGE

Facts and Fancy; how to Keep in Touch with Developments Affecting Securities.

It is always easier to say that the market is going down because it is being raided by powerful and conscienceless bears than merely to call attention to the undoubted fact that no one wants to buy stocks. It not only sounds better; it reads and writes more easily. The writer knows what he is talking about, for he had to fill a column in a New York newspaper with stock market gossip every day for five or six years.

The public must always personify what is going on. There is no way of personifying the cold fact that people do not want to buy stocks, and a financial editor cannot find new ways of stating this naked, unadorned and comfortless truth every day in the year.—ALBERT W. ATWOOD.

THE purpose of the financial page of a newspaper is to reveal the financial situation to the public. And yet, the technical, uninviting, mystifying character of the conventional page would lead one to suspect that the object was to conceal the financial situation.

[182]

Secrets of the Financial Page

Tables with curious symbols unexplained, news stories rendered obscure by Wall Street jargon, parts of the statistical material and text rendered meaningless to the layman by abbreviations—all these traditional characteristics of the old-fashioned financial page tend to repel the inexperienced reader.

By getting the other fellow's point of view and attempting to pity the poor reader the editor can unlock the gates that keep the masses away from the financial page through a few simple changes. If the stories are written in pure lucid English instead of Wall Street journalese, if an explanatory note accompanies statistical tables and explains the key to their workings and their practical utility and, if words are not abbreviated beyond recognition, then the small investor as well as the large can read the financial page with real understanding.

The backbone of the financial page—much as we writers hate to admit it—consists of quotations of prices. The most important of the tables from the standpoint of interest, is that showing dealings in stocks on the New York Stock Exchange and next, dealings in bonds on the New York Stock Exchange, and then transactions on the New York Curb market and quotations in active, unlisted securities.

Many of the New York newspapers start their

[183]

stock quotations with a tabulation of the total volume of transactions in the session reported. The number of sales gives a clue to the extent of speculative interest at the time. In periods of speculative fever, the volume of activity at the great whirlpool of speculation expands, whereas in times of public apathy the number of transactions declines sharply.

A typical record of stock quotations from one of the New York morning newspapers is subjoined:

The first item at the extreme left: *High 1924*—is the highest price which the stock whose name appears slightly to the right has been quoted thus far during the current year. The net item *"Low 1924"* indicates the lowest at which the same stock has been sold during the current year. *"Div. in $"* indicates the regular dividend which the company is paying to shareholders expressed in money, not percentages. After the name of the company the next item is Sales. This figure reveals how many shares of the stock changed hands. An unusually large number of sales for a particular stock lifts it out of the rut and indicates either pool manipulation or active general buying and selling for the expected rise or decline.

The next heading *"Open"* means the first price at which the stock was quoted that day. Although the stock market opens at 10 o'clock sometimes there is

[184]

High. 1924.	Low. 1924.	Div. in $.		Sales.	Open.	High.	Low.	Close.	Net chge.	Bid.	Ask.
82½	73½	6	Adams Express	200	82	82	82	82	+ ¾	81½	82
12½	6	—	Advance Rumely ...	200	8½	9	8½	9	+ ½	8⅝	9¼
41⅛	28¼	3	Advance Rumely pf ..	100	34½	34½	34½	34½	+ 2½	34	35
81½	67¼	4	Air Reduction	200	*79¾	79¾	79⅜	79⅜	+ 1⅛	78	79½
10½	4½	—	Ajax Rubber	300	6⅜	6¾	6⅜	6¾	+ ½	6¼	6¾
1½	⅞	—	Alaska Juneau	300	1¼	1¼	1¼	1¼	——	1¼	1⅜
100	96½	6	All-Amer Cables	100	*99¾	99¾	99¾	99¾	+ 2	98	99¾
74⅝	65	4	Allied Chem & Dye ..	900	73½	73½	72¾	72¾	——	72¾	73⅜
116¼	110	7	Allied Chem & D pf	100	115¾	115¾	115¾	115¾	— ⅛	115	116
50¾	41⅝	4	Allis-Chalmers Mfg ..	1500	50	50¼	49½	50	——	49¾	50½
17	7⅛	—	Amer Agri Chem	100	8¼	8¼	8¼	8¼	+ ¼	8	8½
49½	36	4	Amer Beet Sugar ...	100	41½	41½	41½	41½	——	41	41½
38⅞	22¼	—	Amer Bosch Mag ...	100	30	30	30	30	+ 1½	30	33
122⅝	95⅞	5	American Can	32600	111¼	115¼	110½	115¼	+ 3⅝	115⅛	115¼
115⅞	109	7	Amer Can pf	100	115	115	115	115	——	114½	116
178	153½	12	Amer Car & Fdy	500	162½	164	162½	164	+ 1	164	165
123¾	118¾	7	Amer Car & Fdy pf .	100	123¾	123¾	123¾	123¾	+ ½	124	125
23⅜	21⅜	2	Amer Chain Class A	600	22½	22½	22½	22½	+ ⅝	22½	23
20½	14¾	—	Amer Chicle	700	19⅞	19⅞	19½	19½	——	18½	19½
6¼	3½	—	Amer Drug Synd ...	100	3⅞	3⅞	3⅞	3⅞	— ½	3¾	4¼
107¼	88	6	Amer Express	3700	104	107¼	104	106½	+ 3	105½	106¾
96¼	93	7	Am & For P 25% pf	300	95¾	95¾	95¾	95¾	+ ¾	95½	95¾
96¼	93	7	A & F P 25% pd sel 6	300	95¾	95¾	95¾	95¾	——	95½	95¾
96	86	7	American Ice	300	91	91	90	90	— ½	89⅛	90
1	¼	—	Amer Ice rts	1400	⅞	1	⅞	1	——	—	—
25½	17⅜	—	Amer International .	700	22⅜	22½	22⅜	22½	+ ¾	22¼	22⅜
76⅜	70⅛	6	Amer Locom	1000	74⅞	75	74¾	74¾	— ⅛	74½	74¾
120	116¼	7	Amer Loco pf	100	119½	119½	119½	119½	+ ½	119½	120
45⅞	38¾	3	Amer Metals	200	43¼	43¼	43¼	43¼	+ ¼	42	42¾
107⅛	94¼	4	Amer Radiator	2400	104	106¾	104	106	+ 2¼	106	107
7½	5⅞	.50	Amer Safety Razor ..	200	6⅝	6⅝	6⅝	6⅝	— ⅛	6⅝	7
15⅜	10⅜	—	Amer Ship & Com ..	100	12¼	12¼	12¼	12¼	+ ⅝	12	12½
65¾	57½	5	Amer Smelt & Ref ..	2900	65⅝	65⅝	65	65¼	+ ⅛	65¼	65½
101¼	96	7	Amer S & R pf	100	100¼	100¼	100¼	100¼	— ¾	100¼	101¼
40⅛	33½	3	Amer Steel Fdries ..	1100	35⅝	36¼	35⅝	36	+ ⅜	35¾	36
61¾	38⅝	—	Amer Sugar Ref ..	700	44½	44½	43½	44	— ¼	44	44½
99⅞	79	7	Amer Sugar Ref. pf .	300	87¾	87⅞	87¾	87⅞	+ ⅞	87½	87⅞
130⅞	121⅛	9	Amer Tel & Teleg ..	3400	121⅛	121½	121⅛	121⅜	+ ¼	121¼	121⅜
3$\frac{13}{16}$	2$\frac{15}{16}$	—	Amer Tel & Teleg rts	11384	3½	3$\frac{9}{16}$	3½	3$\frac{9}{16}$	+ $\frac{1}{16}$	3½	3$\frac{9}{16}$
153	135¼	12	Amer Tob Class B ..	500	142¼	142¼	141½	141½	——	141	141¾
88½	40	—	Amer Water W & E	1100	84	84	82	84	——	83¾	84¼
97	**89½**	**7**	**Amer WW&E 1st pf**	**500**	**95⅞**	**96**	**95⅞**	**96**	**——**	**95**	**100**

no transaction in a particular share of stock for two or three hours or even more after the beginning of trading.

As its name indicated, *"High"* signifies the peak price for that stock that day, and *"Low"* precisely the reverse. *"Close"* means the final quotation of a particular share of stock on that day. The stock market on ordinary days closes at 3 o'clock, though frequently the final sale of a particular stock might occur several hours before the end of the trading day. *"Net chge."* meaning net change, signifies the difference between the closing price on the day reported compared with the final price of the previous market. If the final price of the day reported is larger the difference is preceded by a plus sign. If, on the other hand, the final price on the day reported is smaller than on the previous day, the difference is preceded by a minus sign.

Stock prices are quoted in dollars per share.

After net change appear the words *"Bid"* and *"Ask."* Together they give later information on the price situation than the quotation of the final sale. They constitute closing bid and ask prices. The bid is what a buyer is willing to pay for the stock and the ask is the lowest figure which a holder of the stock is willing to sell it for. If the market had not closed, the next sale in all probability would have taken place at some mean figure between the bid and ask prices.

In miscellaneous markets which give quotations of securities that are unlisted on the New York Stock Exchange or on the New York Curb but which are sold actively "over the counter," which means directly by one dealer to another without the formality of transactions on any organized market place, only the bid and ask prices on stocks and the yield on certain classes of bonds are usually reported in the press.

Bonds are quoted in percentages of face values. Newspapers which devote a large amount of space to financial matters continue to report each bond transaction on the New York Stock Exchange separately as the subjoined table indicates.

A sample of a typical Bond Table follows:

N Y City 4s
1956 reg
10.... 98¼
4s 1958
1.... 98¾

A

Adams Expr
4s 1948
1.... 80
Alaska G M cvt
deb 6s
23.... 99⅜
1.... 99½
9.... 99⅜
gold 4s 1948
10.... 86⅞
7.... 86¾
cvt 4½s 1933
1.... 90
2.... 90⅛
1 s5f. 90
1 3d. 90
7.... 90¼
5.... 90
Canadian Gen Elec
deb 6s ser A
1942
4.... 105½
Canadian Nor
6½s 1946
1.... 113⅜
2.... 113½
7s 1940
1.... 113⅜
2.... 113⅝
2.... 113¾
Canadian Pac deb

ser A 1925	
2....	6⅛
Am Ag Ch	
cvt 5s 1928	
1....	96½
7½s 1941	
5....	86
3....	85¾
2....	85½
3....	86
3....	85¾
8....	85½
Am Chain s f	
6s 1933	
5....	94½
1....	94⅞
Am Cot Oil	
5s 1931	
1....	89¾
2....	90
Am D & Imp	
ext 6s 1936	
1....	107¾
Am Republics	
deb 6s 1937	
20....	92¼
Am Sm & Ref	
1st 5s 1947	
19....	94
6s 1947	
1....	105½
2....	105¾
1....	106
Am Sug Ref	
6s 1937	

9....	90
2....	90¼
ref 5s 1995	
5....	85¾
12....	85½
6s 1929	
12....	102½
6....	102¼
1....	102⅜
13....	102½
1....	102¼
8....	102½
2....	102¼
ref & gen 6s	
1995	
5....	101
3....	100⅞
40....	101
1....	101⅛
6....	101
5....	100⅞
2....	101⅛
5....	100⅞
10....	100¾
11....	101
16....	100¾
13....	100⅞
2....	101
P L E & W Va	
4s 1941	
1....	84
2....	83¾
Swn div 3½s	
1925	
22....	99¾

4s perpet	
16....	81¼
1....	80¾
1....	81
5....	80½
Car Clin & O s f	
6s ser A	
1952	
6....	102½
5s 1938	
1....	99
Cen of Ga Ry rf	
& gn 5½s temp	
1959	
4....	98¾
con 5s 1945	
1....	99⅜
Cen Leather 5s	
1925	
85....	99½
Centl Pacific gtd 4s	
1949	
1....	88⅜
10....	88½
12....	88⅜
Centl of N J gen	
6s 1987 reg-	
istered	
1....	105¾
1....	105⅝
Cent R R & Bkg	
Co of Ga col 5s	
1937	
2....	95⅜

At the top of the table these words, *"N Y City 4s 1956 reg 10. . . . 98¼"* mean that ten registered

[188]

bonds representing the obligations of New York City which mature in 1956 and meantime bear interest at the rate of 4% had sold at 98¼% of the face value which in the case of bonds is $1,000. The quotation indicates that such bonds sold at $982.50 each.

Below appears this expression *"Adams Expr. 4s 1948 l. . . . 80."* This of course means that one thousand-dollar bond of the Adams Express Company which falls due in 1948 and meantime bears interest at the rate of 4% had sold at 80% of face value, or $800. Although the maturity date is an essential fact which the investor needs, the newspapers only recently began to include it in their bond tables.[1]

The New York Curb quotations for stocks and bonds, though containing less detail, are based on the same principles as the quotations based on the New York Stock Exchange securities.

Since the war transformed America from a debtor to a creditor nation, interest in international finance has risen markedly.

Reflecting this, the newspapers give greater attention to foreign news and quote the foreign exchanges more fully than in pre-war times.

The subjoined typical foreign exchange table is virtually self-explanatory.

[1] See formula in the appendix for figuring yield on bonds.

EUROPE

	Wednesday	Previous day	Year ago
GREAT BRITAIN (par $4.86 a sovereign)			
Demand	4.53¼	4.53	4.56⅝
Cables	4.53¼	4.53¼	4.56⅞
60-d bills (buy'g)	4.49¾	4.49½	4.53¾
90-d bills (buy'g)	4.48¼	4.48	4.52⅜
FRANCE (par 19.3 cents a franc)			
Demand	5.56	5.54	5.42
Cables	5.56½	5.54½	5.42½
BELGIUM (par 19 cents a franc)			
Demand	5.13½	5.12½	4.42½
Cables	5.14	5.13	4.43
SWITZERLAND (par 19.3 cents a franc)			
Demand	18.86	18.86	18.10
Cables	18.88	18.88	18.13
Italy (par 19.3 cents a lira)			
Demand	4.48¼	4.50¾	4.28½
Cables	4.48½	4.51	4.29
Holland (par 40.2 cents a florin)			
Demand	39.05	39.02	39.27
Cables	39.09	39.06	39.31
AUSTRIA (par 20.3 cents a crown)			
Demand	.0014⅛	.0014⅛	.0014
Cables	.0014⅛	.0014⅛	.0014
NORWAY (par 26.8 cents a crown)			
Demand	13.97	13.92	16.65
Cables	13.99	13.94	16.68
SWEDEN (par 26.8 cents a crown)			
Demand	26.61	26.58	26.65
Cables	26.63	26.60	26.68
DENMARK (par 26.8 cents a crown)			
Demand	16.12	16.04	18.64
Cables	16.12	16.06	18.67
SPAIN (par 19.3 cents a peseta)			
Demand	13.49	13.50	13.64
Cables	13.51	13.52	13.66

Secrets of the Financial Page

The "Demand" quotation is that on checks that are sent across the seas by ordinary mail. The quotation for "cables" is for instantaneous transfer of funds by cable or wireless. The quotations for 60 and 90 day bills are for commercial paper which becomes payable 60 or 90 days after presentation at a foreign bank. The varying periods of availability of the cash entailed in these four types of quotations make allowance at current interest rates for loss of use of funds in the meantime.

The subjoined table indicates the status of the money market, which, in turn, has an important bearing on the speculative and commercial situation.

MONEY AND CREDIT

CALL LOANS

Renew	2	Last	2
High	2	Previous close	2
Low	2	Year ago	6

TIME LOANS

	Mixed	Industrials.
Sixty days	2½@ —	2½@ —
Ninety days	2½@2¾	2½@2¾
Four to six months	3 @3½	3 @3½

COMMERCIAL PAPER

Best names, four to six months	3½
Other names, four to six months	4

Common Sense of Money and Investments

Thirty days...	2⅛ @ 2
Sixty days...	2⅛ @ 2—
Ninety days...	2⅛ @ 2—
Four months...	2⅛ @ 2—
Five months...	2½ @ 2⅜
Six months...	2½ @ 2⅜
Call loans...	1½ @ 1¾

Call loans are one-day loans by which brokers borrow funds from banks and put up stocks and bonds listed on the New York Stock Exchange as collateral. Such loans are made only for a single day, but can be renewed by mutual consent for an indefinite period. Sometimes call loans run for five or six years. The most significant rate is the renewal rate.

Time loans, as the term is used in the foregoing table, constitute another means by which brokers borrow funds from banks to finance speculative customers who buy securities on margin; that is, who put up only 10, 20 or 30 per cent or more of the cost of the securities and instruct their brokers to pay the rest. Time loans are the same as call loans except that instead of running for one day they continue for a definite stipulated period, such as 60, 90 or 180 days.

Commercial paper and "Bankers' Acceptances" reflect not speculative operations in securities but actual financing of trade by business men. In addition to borrowing at their own banks, a number of larger business enterprises also sell their short term promises to pay, usually running up to six months, to so-called bill brokers who in turn sell the notes to banks and others seeking short term investments. Bankers' acceptances are similar but differ in one essential respect. They carry not only the promise of one concern to pay, but always at least two names including that of a bank. An acceptance is a bill of exchange drawn by the seller of merchandise on the buyer, who gets a bank to signify in his behalf acceptance of the obligation to pay. If the buyer signifies acceptance directly instead of through a bank, the bill becomes known as a trade acceptance, instead of a bankers' acceptance. Trade acceptances are used primarily in domestic trade, whereas bankers acceptances are ordinarily used to finance shipments of commodities to foreign countries.

Statistical material and routine constitute a large and important part of a financial page. The originality and enterprise of the financial editor are reflected in the character of the statistical material, but good innovations are quickly copied by his competitors. The actual reading matter, consisting of financial editorials and news stories, better reflects the real personality of the editor and his staff. The ordinary financial page starts with the so-called market lead, in which the financial editor comments on the significance of the day's fluctuations at the security and commodity exchanges. He attempts in this article also to interpret the speculative significance of domestic and world news of a political and economic character. In his leading article he strives to rationalize about the seemingly chaotic and sometimes meaningless minor movements in speculative prices. He strives to give life and significance to the statistical material which abounds on the financial pages.

On the same page as the stock quotations and the market lead, there usually appears a so-called gossip column which runs under sundry headings in the Metropolitan newspapers, such as "In Wall Street," "Topics in Wall Street," "Wall Street Talk," "The Day in the Street," and "News for Investors."

Whereas the market lead deals with the markets as a whole, these paragraphs treat of particular securities and commodities. They reflect the chatter of brokerage offices, much of which needs to be sifted critically.

Carefully edited newspapers do not wish to be used by pool manipulators to disseminate misleading information designed to lure suckers into their snares. And yet paragraphs conveying gossip rather than authentic or official information, should be read in the spirit of criticism and challenge. Gossip columns frequently give the first intimation of new developments before they have been formulated into definite announcements which constitute formal news stories. In speculative matters time is of the essence and the astute trader who can build up speculative theories from mere hints will prefer an inkling to-day to an exhaustive story to-morrow. When a company is ready to make an official announcement concerning new developments the speculative value of the information has usually already been capitalized. On the ordinary financial page the gossip column is the most distinctly speculative feature.

Standards vary on different newspapers as to the care with which material for the gossip column is gathered. In some newspapers, less exacting than others, the gossip column constitutes an admixture of fact and fancy where the theories of reporters, brokers, and professional speculators are exploited. Even some newspapers that are exceedingly careful in their news stories and in the editorial material, let down the bars somewhat in the treatment of gossip paragraphs.

Reports of the grain exchanges, the cotton market and the Curb embody some of the principles of the stock market lead, entailing a factual report of the day's transactions combined with an editorial interpretation of the meaning of the changes. However, they ordinarily occupy less space and are done by subordinates rather than by the chief of staff. They run either under stock heads such as "Curb Market" "Cotton Market," "Grain Market," or under ordinary news headlines, which feature the peculiar character of the day's transactions. Besides these there are on the ordinary financial pages a variety of financial news stories depending on the events of the day.

Broadly speaking, two kinds of news stories appear on the financial pages,—news of cause and news of effect. Under news of effect may be grouped the stock market lead, the curb story and the articles about the cotton and grain exchanges, all of which chronicle the result of new and prospective developments on security prices.

News of cause, on the other hand, consists of stories containing information which will react on security or commodity prices. It is news of this character that speculators are particularly anxious to get, for it is the stuff out of which their plans and strategies are made. News of effect constitute regular everyday routine features. Under news of cause, an enterprising newspaper may carry exclusive stories.

The various bank statements [2] open up to public

[2] For an explanation of the meaning of the bank statements, see Chap. XX.

view the status of money markets. At present the statements published in the newspaper on Fridays of the twelve Federal Reserve Banks and combined system are the most important of the bank statements. The next most significant are the statements published on Saturday mornings on the condition of the member banks of the Federal Reserve system and those published Saturday afternoon and Sunday morning on the status of members of the clearing house of New York and other cities.

The real use of the financial page to the investor is that it offers him a convenient means of keeping in touch with developments that affect the value of his securities. In this fluid changing world where revolutions and new industrial methods quickly render old ways obsolete, it is ordinarily poor policy to buy securities and lock them up in a safe deposit vault and forget them. The prudent investor, especially when holding anything but high grade securities, will seek to follow the changing panorama of finance and to determine the effect of altering conditions on his own investment list.

Unlike the speculator who is perpetually shifting his holdings, the investor will do well to hold on to what he has until there is good reason for making a change. However, there are occasions when wisdom entails getting out of one security and into another. For example, industrial corporations depend for their success, to a very large extent, on the character of management. Sometimes the controlling groups will yield to a new element which proves less capable. The effect of inferior direction will ultimately be reflected in the earnings of the company which are reported on the financial page.

The investor automatically receives periodic reports from companies in which he is a stock holder or registered bond holder, but does not get reports of companies in which he holds coupon bonds. Moreover he can frequently find interim indications of earnings only in the newspapers.

All these reports and more he will find on the financial page of a comprehensive newspaper. Moreover, he is interested not only in the company to which he has entrusted funds, but also potentially in all other companies which might offer good opportunities. The financial pages open various vistas and keep him in touch with the financial status of all the more significant railroad, industrial, and public utility corporations.

With the development of the small investor [3] new features have been added to the financial page. A very important one is the investment column in which specific investment problems presented by readers

[3] See Foreword.

[198]

are answered. Potentially, this feature can be of very large service to the financial community, but its utility depends largely on the skill with which it is handled. [4]

There is also among more progressive newspapers a drift toward personal journalism on the financial page. Feature writers in daily columns comment on the passing show in finance. The better of these columns are written by men with an individual style of expression and with the gift of a human interest touch. They frequently give information about men as well as purely statistical facts. They take the raw material of the day's news and tie it up to the problems and interests of the general reader, giving the meaning of the news as well as the bare facts.

Other important information on the financial page is contained in paid advertisements. In the past, careless newspapers permitted fakers, charlatans and bucketeers to enter their advertising columns. The more alert publishers, however, were on their guard and recently there has prevailed, particularly among the metropolitan newspapers, higher standards in regard to selecting financial advertising. A reputable publisher now will accept financial advertising only from those in whose integrity he has positive reason to believe. Border line cases should be placed on

[4] See Chap. XIX. "Some Fallacies of the Investment Column."

the defensive and kept out until they have proved their dependability. The financial advertising columns of a newspaper should be a trustworthy guide from which readers can select honest brokers.

One important function of financial advertising is to announce new security creations. Even the most exacting newspaper will accept speculative as well as investment offerings, provided the bankers indicate truthfully the nature of their offering.

Since investing in the last decade became a mass instead of a class activity, financial advertising has improved greatly in clarity and human interest, but it is still in a primitive stage compared with more highly developed merchandising copy in the mercantile field. All except the more progressive financial advertisers still confuse dullness with dignity and barrenness with truthfulness.

The New York Stock Exchange, in a laudable effort to protect the public, imposes taboos on its members in respect to advertising which tend to frustrate its use as a selling force. Though the stock exchange's purpose is praiseworthy, its technique has been faulty, although progress is being made. Good institutional advertising can be made a force for public education.

[200]

CHAPTER XIX

SOME FALLACIES OF THE INVESTMENT COLUMN

The Need of Speculation; Price and Yield some-time a Delusive Guide to Safety.

If uncertainty were avoided by withdrawing capital from all investments in which more than the minimum degree of risk is involved, society would suffer a great diminution in well-being. The fact that capital can obtain the extra reward necessary to induce it to enter a hazardous employment shows that society prefers to bear the extra expense rather than content itself with the products of safe investments.—A. H. WILLETT.

If the avoidance of risk proceeds to the point of eliminating risk entirely, profits, instead of being increased, are annihilated; for that implies an abandonment of the venture.—F. B. HAWLEY.

THE investment column in well conducted newspapers, in which specific questions of readers are answered, is a service station for the security buyer. It can render significant aid to the investor and lead him into channels of safety and profit. It can offset the exaggerations of over-zealous security salesmen. It can correct the false perspectives of bond circulars and stock prospectuses. It has an opportunity to focus public attention on the unseemly aspects of a would-be borrowing corporation, whereas security venders, in the process of hawking their wares, naturally stress the favorable side.

The investment column can subtly warn readers of new frauds before complete legal proof of wrongdoing has been built up. It can reveal the hazards and costs of speculation. It can help to take its regular readers off sucker lists. It can assist readers to check emotional impulses in selecting securities and guide them in the spirit of scientific analysis.

But the investment column of a newspaper of large circulation is necessarily intended primarily for the average investor. The requirements of industry, however, depend not only on the average man but also on the extraordinary individual who can see opportunities as they first rise dimly on the industrial horizon and who is endowed with sufficient financial intelligence and monetary resources to assume the special risks involved in financing new and experimental ideas.

"Safety First," the motto of the investment column, constitutes a good standard of action for the individual of small means who cannot afford to lose.

Some Fallacies of the Investment Column

Yet safety in the investment world—always a relative concept—would be impossible of attainment if venturesome individuals did not supply the marginal funds which absorb the greater risks.

Industry is subject to the law of incessant flux. Progress is made in business through trial and error and ceaseless experiment. The Andrew Carnegies of industry adjust themselves to the sweep of marching events by scrapping colossal plants as they become obsolete and more efficient substitutes are found.

Risk is inherent in trade, for the calculations of the business man depend largely on his reading of the future which is necessarily to a large extent unknowable. In supplying the financial sinews to enterprises whose fortunes necessarily ebb and flow, the security buyer is consciously taking greater risks than are involved in buying high grade government bonds, but he is doing so under the stimulus of the hope of greater returns than can be obtained from safe investment.

The advice of the well-edited investment columns is good as far as it goes, but it should not be looked upon as the formulation of a system of political economy. Business needs venturesome capital and the spirit of adventure.

Moreover, the advice to buy safe bonds only is not

[203]

at all times and at all places good advice. In times of inflation and rising commodity prices, the individual whose funds are invested solely in sound bonds will suffer a loss in purchasing power and at least temporarily in the market value of his securities. Whereas in such circumstances if he has a large portion of his funds in the shares of well managed and prosperous business corporations, his securities will rise proportionately with the general level of prices and will offset any disadvantages to him in general inflation.

Conversely, in times of falling commodity prices, the holder of bonds will fare relatively better than the holder of stock.[1]

Furthermore, the investment editor must be perpetually on his guard against the temptation to believe that low yield and safety always go hand in hand. It is true that a return on securities far above the current basic interest rate constitutes a warning of possible danger and that a low yield close to the pure interest rate tends to indicate safety. At least the market price and yield reflect the collective judgmen of men who buy and sell securities at the market place. But the expert can not depend on mass judgment. Price, he will find, reflects not only intrinsic

[1] For fuller discussion, see Chapter XI, "When to Switch from Stocks to Bonds."

[204]

worth, but also popular whims, fancies, and fashions.

Low yields sometimes lead the investor to disaster. Russian and Turkish bonds which sold on a 4 per cent yield basis and were seemingly conservative have defaulted on principal and interest. Local bonds of ferry companies operating in New York City waters were once looked upon as gilt edged investments. The building of bridges and tunnels offered unexpected competition to these old ferry lines, some of which were driven out of existence.

Bonds of street car lines have been especially hard pressed during the last decade, through limitations in fares, iron clad franchise and competition from motor buses. New York Railways 4s, for example, which sold at 79 in 1913 and were considered a fair investment at that time declined to 15½ in 1920; the 5s of 1945 which were marketed at 103¼ in 1913 were available at 25 in 1921.

In the domestic railroad field New York, New Haven & Hartford 4 per cent issues sold above their face value a decade ago. They have since receded to 36, although there has been some recovery recently. The securities of this road suffered from over development of the system, unwise investments in trolleys and other property not needed for the operation of the railroad system, and from the failure of the New England territory to keep pace with the industrial growth of the country generally. Furthermore, Chicago, Milwaukee & St. Paul 4½ per cent mortgage bonds which once had the highest rating have slumped to around 60 in recent years, compared with 106⅜ in 1913. An extension to the Pacific Coast which has not, up to this time, become definitely profitable and an agricultural depression in a region where too much mileage existed were the principal causes of the setback.

In general, fallacies of investment columns are largely errors of interpretation, for which the reader rather than the writer is responsible. A piece of advice should be weighed in connection with the particular question. It constitutes a reply to an individual query, rather than the exposition of a universal truth.

CHAPTER XX

THE STORY BEHIND THE FIGURES IN A FINANCIAL REPORT

What to Look for in a Balance Sheet and an Income Account.

Reports tell management when business is sick, before it dies, and management is expected to restore health.—A. R. ERSKINE.

The selling value of shares should be, apparently, the book value of the assets minus the liabilities. Yet, no matter how accurately the assets may be valued and the liabilities ascertained, it is very seldom that the selling price corresponds to the book value. The purchaser is buying for future income, and will not invest unless he sees a prospect of getting it.—CHARLES E. SPRAGUE.

IN the drab statements which a corporation distributes to its share holders from one to twelve times a year is hidden a story of immense value. The individual who can read a financial report intelligently is able to observe at first hand the fluctuating fate of the enterprise to which he has entrusted his thrift funds.

[207]

Common Sense of Money and Investments

The man who can find illumination in a study of official reports is less subject to the hysteria of the market place—less prone to heed the rumors and tips that fly around the financial district than the gullible individual who throws statements of the company into the wastebasket and bases his investment procedure on hearsay and gossip.

A lucidly drawn up financial statement ought not to elude the grasp of the layman who has studied the anatomy of a company report. The lay investor of ordinary intelligence who is willing to give a little study to the matter can soon learn the key by which he can discover the story of success or failure in the emotionless statistics.

To the trained eye slight alterations in significant items foreshadow broad drifts either toward increased prosperity or toward recession.

Honestly drawn up financial statements reveal early symptoms of financial disease which competent management will be quick to relieve. To be of utmost value, statements of earnings ought to be prepared with celerity and made available to executives promptly.

If all stock holders are to be placed on an equal footing with the management with respect to important financial information, it is necessary to publish frequent reports of the earnings and expenses,

[208]

Story Behind the Figures in a Report

(monthly wherever feasible). Corporations which conceal such information from their stock holders until months after the year has closed present, in their tardy annual statements, ancient history of little speculative value. The great body of stock holders are subject to exploitation on the part of insiders of corporations which do not issue regular financial reports promptly.

The balance sheet of a corporation reveals the condition of an enterprise on a given day—usually December 31st.

The balance sheet is a cross section view of a corporation at a particular moment in its history.

An income account, on the other hand, reveals profits or losses during a given period. A balance sheet is static, an income account dynamic. The two together, if honestly conceived, indicate the status of a corporation.

At best, a financial report is a statement of opinion. Value is a subjective concept and the worth of assets as stated on the balance sheet unless actual cost is used, is subject to individual variation.

In financial statements all is relative. To-day's balance sheet becomes significant when set against that of a year ago. Without comparison the items in a financial statement have little meaning.

A representative financial statement follows:

[209]

Common Sense of Money and Investments

Balance Sheet

Assets

Current:	1923	Dec. 31, 1922
Cash	$6,458,683	$2,216,678
A/cs.	17,253,042	10,497,234
Bills receivable	3,646,442	7,012,871
Marketable securities	880,914	561,983
Foreign Govt. securities	18,468,431	20,010,108
Inventories	5,154,511	10.855,176
Total current	51,862,023	51,154,050
Plant and Equip. less depre.	29,309,690	26,898,185
Investments	7,445,715	7,436,163
Deferred charges	538,977	418,927
Mtge. bonds held in sinking fund	2,272,125	1,968,225
	91,428,530	87,875,550

Liabilities

Current:	1923	1922
Accounts payable	3,203,775	6,370,582
Savings fund for employees	1,818,179	1,594,236
Accrued interest	528,582	579,511
Bills payable	4,500,000	5,000,000
Reserve on account of contr.	....	549,000
Total current	10,050,536	14,093,329
Preferred stock	20,000,000	20,000,000
Common stock	20,000,000	20,000,000
Mortgage bonds	10,000,000	10,000,000
Reserve for deferred items	4,192,363	4,359,375
Reserve for removals and taxes	4,538,389	492,068
Reserve for 1924 dividends	2,800,000	....
Surplus	19,847,242	18,930,778
	91,428,530	87,875,550

Story Behind the Figures in a Report

INCOME ACCOUNT

The Baldwin Locomotive Works

	1923	Dec. 31, 1922
Gross sales	$102,762,075	$33,087,259
Cost of sales	92,577,320	31,092,897
Gross Profit	10,184,755	1,994,362
Other income	2,912,844	6,078,574
Total income	13,097,599	8,072,936
Deduct—		
Interest and removal	1,166,077	1,307,422
Tax reserves	4,400,000	300,000
Depreciation reserves	600,000	600,000
Reserve for deferred profits	415,058	658,995
Total deductions	6,581,135	2,866,417
Net income	6,516,464	5,206,519
Preferred dividends	1,400,000	1,400,000
Common dividends	1,400,000	1,400,000
Surplus for year	3,716,464	2,406,519
Previous Surplus	18,930,778	13,257,534
Total surplus	22,647,242	15,664,053
On preferred	32.58	26.03
On Common	25.58	19.03

The foregoing tables constitute the financial reports of a typical large American industrial corporation. Such items as deferred charges and accrued interest may generally be ignored as they represent mainly adjustments necessary to give a current static

[211]

cross section of the condition of a company whose affairs flow in an unbroken stream through the date on which the statements are made up.

In the ordinary balance sheet the amount of cash on hand should be compared with previous years. A marked decline, unless there has been an extraordinary advance in prices, is a danger signal, especially if accompanied by an unduly large increase in inventory which represents goods on hand. Surplus is perhaps not as important an item as the uninformed believe, since it is possible to build up a fictitious surplus by juggling with figures. The investor should seek to ascertain whether the item represents genuine tangible assets. The item appearing on the liability side of the balance sheet indicates an excess of assets over liabilities. The assets consist of a list of the sources of wealth of the corporation. The liabilities, on the other hand, entail a list of the obligations of the corporation either to outsiders or to its own stockholders.

The first item among the fixed assets is ordinarily "real estate and plant." In this connection it is important to know *what is the basis of the valuation and what allowance has been made for depreciation. To replace worn out buildings or obsolete machinery a depreciation fund is set aside out of earnings and as such cannot be disbursed to stockholders.*

[212]

Story Behind the Figures in a Report

If the depreciation fund is larger than the known decline in value of property it is sometimes carried on the liability side, representing an accumulation of net profits which the corporation really owes to its stockholders. An excess over known depreciation constitutes an insurance fund against future declines in property values. Sometimes the item appears both on the asset and liability side, but where it appears only on the liability side the depreciation fund consists of general assets without particular designation. Other similar items are reserve funds against various contingencies, insurance funds, and retirement funds.

Another significant item on the balance sheet is bills receivable, consisting of promissory notes of the commercial debtors of the corporation. Deductions from their face value should be made in cases where the probability of collection is doubtful. To go behind the figure itself it is necessary to inspect the actual bills and ascertain the nature of the debtors. A bank lending money to a corporation will frequently undertake to do this. The item—accounts receivable—is about the same as bills receivable except that it represents commercial debts recorded on the books of the creditor, but not acknowledged in promissory notes or acceptances. These items will vary in accordance with the seasons. According to

Common Sense of Money and Investments

Professor William Morse Cole, in some lines of business back accounts will average 60 per cent uncollectable and on others only 80 per cent on the average will be collectable.

Inventory consists of goods or merchandise on hand and the balance sheet should indicate whether it has been figured at the original cost or present market value. *It is good practice to take whichever basis is lower.* Only the lowest net figures of cost after all discounts have been subtracted should be used. Allowance should be made for merchandise depreciation because of changing fashions, loss in handling breakage, and shop wear. Appraisers estimate the actual value of merchandise in different lines of business all the way from 50 per cent of cost to 95 per cent of cost. Groceries do not depreciate rapidly, whereas dry goods, millinery and furs change quickly in value.

On the liability side of the balance sheet appears the item capital stock, representing what the corporation owes to its own shareholders. This is a theoretical obligation which remains in perpetuity and which causes the directors of a corporation little concern. The figure represents the total amount of stock outstanding.

On the other hand, bond obligations appear on the balance sheet representing genuine obligations which some day must be paid off and for which provision must be made in handling the funds of an enterprise.

Bills payable represent debts of the corporation, usually merchandise or current operations to outsiders for which notes or acceptances acknowledging the debt have been given. Accounts payable represent similar obligations for which no notes or acceptances have been given.

Profit and loss, or loss and gain, or surplus or undivided profits in the liability column constitute a mere bookkeeping device representing an excess of resources over specific recognized liabilities. It is fundamental in accounting that nothing can be increased or decreased on the liability side without an equivalent change on the asset side. To quote Professor Cole again: [1] "It is evident in the first place that an increase in a resource account (assets) indicates that something has been spent to acquire that increased resource. Similarly a decrease in a liability account indicates the same sort of thing, for the liability must have been paid off and therefore something has been spent. Conversely, a decrease in a resource account indicates that something has been taken from this account during the year and spent elsewhere; or what amounts to the same thing, this

[1] See his "Accounts: Their Construction and Interpretation."

[215]

decrease is part of an exchange of one asset for another. Similarly, again, the increase in a liability account indicates that the firm has borrowed some sort of property and hence it by so much has had means to spend. By making a comparison, then, of balance sheets, tabulating the increases and decreases of resources and liabilities, we can see from what sources all receipts came and to what destinations all expenditures went. In making this tabulation, we may well give any one of three titles to each column. Let us call the first column credits, or receipts, or 'Where got'; the second column we may call debits, or expenditures, or 'Where gone.' Clearly if any account on any side of the balance sheet remains at the same figure as the preceding year, however many transactions may have taken place in that account, we need take no thought of them, for the net result was to leave the account as before; so we are concerned only with changes."

To ascertain from a study of the balance sheet the well being of a corporation, assets and liabilities should be examined with the time element in mind. For a corporation with a superabundance of assets might get into serious financial difficulties if its liabilities, though small, soon became payable, whereas its assets, though large, cannot be realized upon for a relatively long period. Accordingly the discerning student of the balance sheet compares so-called quick assets with current liabilities. These distinctions attempt to draw the line between short term and long term items. A prosperous corporation should have ordinarily two or three times as many quick assets as liabilities. Under quick assets would be included cash, bills and accounts receivable, and merchandise or inventory. Current liabilities include bills payable, accounts payable, bank loans, and any notes or bonds maturing within the next few months.

A railroad report is ordinarily divided into three parts: a balance sheet or general account; an income sheet or income account; and the traffic report or statistics. True interpretation comes from a grouping of all three in relation to one another.

Under the uniform accounting regulations of the Interstate Commerce Commission there are fewer individual differences in the form of drawing up reports than in those of industrial corporations. As a sweeping generalization, it is safe to say that railroad reports on account of outside regulation, are more dependable than industrial reports.

The balance sheet embodies the same principles as that of an industrial corporation.

In the income account, the term—*"gross earnings"*—is usually employed to designate sums received for services rendered including passenger, freight, mail and express and miscellaneous services. "Operating expenses" represent the expenses incurred in obtaining the gross earnings. The relation of such expenses to gross income is called the operating ratio and the size of the ratio is a good index to the efficiency with which the property is managed. An operating ratio of more than 80 per cent is likely to indicate inefficiency.

To gross earnings "other income," which includes receipts from investments and from sale of capital assets, is added and the total represents "gross income." From this figure, fixed charges including interest on bonds, taxes, and other items dependent on operating expense must be deducted. After fixed charges have been subtracted from gross income the result is the amount earned and is available for dividends. Any excess not paid out to share holders in the form of dividends is transferred to surplus account.

The accounting systems of public utility corporations are subject to regulation by State Commissions and in general principles resemble the forms of railroad accounting.

Where unusual terms are used on the balance sheet or income account, or vague expressions are employed, a conscientious accountant will explain them in accompanying statements. Where no such

[218]

explanation is offered, the company exposes itself to the suspicion that it is deliberately trying to conceal from stockholders significant information and the investor will do well to eschew the securities of such enterprises. It is always a good rule to keep away from the securities of corporations which do not at least comply with the minimum requirements of the New York Stock Exchange for an annual statement showing earnings and expenses and a balance sheet.

In the balance sheet of promotion companies the items—*"investments or securities owned"*—are frequently difficult of precise valuation by the outsider. The balance sheet should indicate clearly what the investments consist of. The investments of the Union Pacific Railroad for instance, which are carried at more than $230,000,000, consist of first mortgages, railroad bonds, and equipment trust obligations and preferred and common stock of important railroads throughout the country. In some instances the company values its holdings below their actual market quotations. It is conservative practice to carry such investments at either cost or market prices, whichever happen to be lower.

Where investments consist of holdings of unmarketable securities of subsidiary corporations, the item is arbitrary and frequently is the hidden cause of financial troubles. The investments of the "L. R.

[219]

Steel Company, Inc.," for example, which recently went into receivership, consisted almost entirely of unmarketable securities of affiliated companies, making purchase of the stock equivalent to buying a cat in a bag.

Another item among assets of promotion companies which is frequently a source for concealing water is the item of good will or patents or franchise— the so-called intangible items.

Good will represents the reputation or standing of the enterprise in the business world, undoubtedly a thing of real worth. However, it is a paradox of business that those concerns with genuine good will, for reasons of conservatism, carry it at little or nothing among their assets, whereas those without real good will have an inflated item under that heading on the balance sheet. Banks which possess a reputation of great value do not carry items of this nature in their statements. Moreover, the Eastman Kodak Co., whose trade name and patents are of colossal value, does not include these items among its assets. The General Electric Company values its numerous and enormously valuable patents and franchises at one dollar.

On the other hand, mercantile enterprises including department stores and chain stores usually carry good will at a comparatively high figure, but even

[220]

among well managed concerns of this kind there is a tendency to reduce rather than inflate the intangible items. The F. W. Woolworth Co., for instance, gradually wrote down its good will from $50,000,000 to $20,000,000 in 1923 and intends eventually to eliminate this item.

The investor should beware of the new concern which carries good will, patents, organization expenses, and similar items at large figures on its balance sheet, for they are receptacles of water.

In connection with the inventory figure among the assets, it is important to ascertain the rate of turnover, which shows how many times the stocks on hand were sold during the year. By dividing the inventory figure on the balance sheet into the annual amount of sales the number of times the stock has been turned over may be learned. Ordinarily the turnover of a mercantile concern will be greater than that of a manufacturing enterprise. A sharp slowing up in turnover is a signal of danger. If sales decline while inventories rise, it is apparent that the concern is loaded up with unmovable merchandise which usually foretells a loss.

In the reports accompanying the statistics of well managed corporations are remarks by the president or chairman of the board of directors who seeks to interpret and explain the significance of the various items. A chief executive who neglects this opportunity to clarify the situation for shareholders is genuinely open to criticism. If he is trying honestly to serve the great body of stockholders, he will use the reports as an occasion for letting in the light of publicity and will avoid no means of clarifying obscure points. The small investor should not hesitate to write to the chief executive of a company in which he is interested for an explanation of items that do not seem crystal clear.

Statements of national state banks vary somewhat from those of industrial corporations. The most significant items of a balance sheet of a financial institution are capital, surplus and undivided profits, loans and investments of gross deposits. The ratio of capital, surplus and undivided profits to the amount of its deposits indicate the degree of protection for creditors. Moreover, the shareholders of national banks and of virtually all state banks are liable to an amount equal to the par value of their shares to satisfy the claims of the depositers.

The total amount of loans and investments represents the commercial paper, gold notes, bonds, stocks and other assets of value which have been bought with the capital of the bank and the funds of depositors. Discounted paper is ordinarily carried at its face value on the asset side of the balance sheet. The offsetting item "reserve for unearned discount" on the liability side reduces the value of the notes to their true worth on the date on which the statement is compiled.

"Cash in reserve" represents the amount which the bank is required to retain in lawful money or keep on deposit with an approved institution as protection for its depositors.

To the investor who attempts to diagnose general economic conditions the most important of bank statements is the weekly combined statement of the twelve Federal Reserve Banks which is published every Friday morning in the press. The reserve ratio, which represents the percentage of reserves to deposits and notes in circulation, usually declines in times of business activity and increasing prices, and rises in periods of receding business and declining commodity prices.

"Bills Discounted" include commercial paper eligible for rediscount. A member bank which has to increase its deposits with the reserve institution will present eligible bills for rediscount with instructions that the proceeds be credited to its account. The reserves carried by members constitute the total of the "member banks—reserve account" item on the liability side of the balance sheet. Under the Federal Reserve Act every member of the system is required to

carry a certain percentage of its deposits (average about 10 per cent) in the form of a credit balance with the reserve bank in the territory in which it is situated. An increase in the deposits of member banks usually accompanies a rise in the balances of their own customers who are the business men of the community. A perusal of the *"bills discounted"* item will ordinarily reveal whether the increased deposits of member banks at the central bank represent an accumulation of cash or an increase in borrowing.

The gold reserve is divided into various accounts. "Gold with the Federal Reserve Agent" is designated for the redemption of circulating notes. The gold settlement fund which reposes in Washington in the custody of the Federal Reserve Board allows for the settlement of claims of one Federal Reserve Bank against another by a process of bookkeeping without the physical shipment of metal.

"Federal Reserve Notes and Surplus" represent a significant part of the nation's circulating medium. An increase of the quantity of notes outstanding is ordinarily a signal either that the volume of trade is expanding or that prices are rising, or both.

Prior to the formation of the Federal Reserve System, a deficit in reserves revealed in the weekly statement of the New York Clearing House which is published at noon on Saturday was looked upon as a serious warning of stringency money conditions, whereas an adequate surplus of reserves indicated an abundance of credit. These items in the Clearing House statement have to a large extent lost their significance under the operation of the Federal Reserve System because if the banks now show a deficit in reserves they can immediately correct the situation by rediscounting bills at the Federal Reserve Bank. The fundamentally important test of the credit situation is the status of the Federal Reserve System. If any one of the twelve regional banks is hard pressed it can immediately get funds from one or all of the other eleven banks by rediscounting paper with them.

When the Clearing House statement reveals a deficit in reserves, a temporary tightening of call money rates may be expected on the next business day. Increasing activity in securities is usually accompanied by a rapid expansion in the loan account and a more gradual increase in deposits. Periods of dullness in the security markets usually go hand in hand with an increase in the ratio of deposits to loans.

CHAPTER XXI

SOOTHSAYERS IN WALL STREET

A Critical Survey of the Art and Science of Financial Forecasting; why Tips are Misleading.

There is no reason to believe the business forecast is more accurate than the weather forecast. Yet, though storm indications are not always borne out, it pays well in the long run for the market gardener to regard them; a somewhat vague promise of a cold snap without the exact hour, temperature, or duration specified is better than nothing. To heed the indications of trouble or the promises of recovery is business common sense.—WESLEY CLAIR MITCHELL.

Viewing the disastrous phenomenon of boom and slump in the light of what the government can properly do, I believe there has been a great underestimation as to the potential importance to commerce and industry of an adequate service of statistics. I believe that the stability and soundness of business can be greatly enhanced, and vicious speculation can be curtailed, by a more adequate information service. We should have more timely, more regular, and more complete information of the current production and consumption and stocks of the great commodities in the United States.—HERBERT HOOVER.

Soothsayers in Wall Street

For centuries man, limited to a knowledge of the past and present, has striven to peer into the future and learn the secrets of the Deity.

The quest for a crystal ball in which important events can be foreseen goes endlessly on. The demand for fortune tellers and soothsayers appears to be eternal.

The oracles of Ancient Greece attracted the greatest soldiers and statesmen to them. Like all successful fortune tellers the oracles prospered through the trick of generalization, stirring the imagination of the subject and leaving him to fill in the details around the skeleton of prophecy which was broad enough to cover virtually any contingencies. Cæsar was skeptical and ignored the soothsayer's warning to "beware the Ides of March," but endless generations of superstitious folk have since been impressed with the occult power of fortune tellers and have searched for similar guidance and warning.

The chief preoccupation of contemporary civilization is industry and trade and the most significant present day prophets therefore are those prognosticators who feel that they have the key to the secrets of the future of commerce and finance. Dependable advance information, if obtainable, would be of far-reaching importance to the investor, for it would guide him in the selection of securities that would prosper and would deflect him from stocks and bonds destined to wither and fade into obscurity. To the business man, knowledge about the future would be of no less value, for it would enable him to know the amount of future demand for merchandise and would eliminate the great risk of producing in advance against needs which are necessarily problematical. Economic forecasting, a new science or pseudo science, opens up enormous possibilities for substituting calm reason for chaos in the business world.

Yet the future is to a large extent unknowable. The factor of accidents looms so large that the events of the future in any exact sense seem predestined to remain the secrets of the gods. However, though unknowable, for business purposes, the events of the future—in at least an approximate sense—must be foreseen. The business man and the security buyer, guiding themselves by past records and experiences, base their decisions mainly on a theory as to what is likely to occur in the future.

Floods, earthquakes, famines, war, pestilences, and other unpredictable events recur to remind each generation of the fallibility of its prejudgment of the future. At best, even if made on the basis of a more scientific technique than any that has yet been devised, business forecasts can be no more than tentative and approximate statements of what events are likely to flow from certain causes or premises. The naïve persons who think that by subscribing $100 a year to a statistical service they can eliminate every element of risk and uncertainty from the future are gullible indeed. Well conducted statistical services which have made expert examination of the factors affecting trade and finance can at best give background and systematic indications of what is likely to occur, provided expected influences operate and are not offset by accidental factors which have not been anticipated.

A distinction should be made between mere guesses as to what the future will bring and the kind of prophecy now known as business forecasting. Druidic priests in ancient Britain made prophecies concerning the weather, but they were hardly comparable to the daily bulletins of the United States Weather Bureau, although their aims were precisely the same. What the modern prophet of business seeks to do is to apply the net result of economic science and the knowledge of economic laws to the problem of determining from current conditions in which direction the trend of business and prices is turning.

Business forecasting, still in an experimental state, has not attained the dignity of a precise science. Business forecasts are accurate in the same sense that the weather forecast is. It all depends upon how much allowance is made for the element of time. When the weather bureau predicts fair weather, it is always right, although it is sometimes necessary to wait four days to a week for the prophecy to come true. Predictions of fair business weather are equally likely to be realized if one is sufficiently patient. But for practical purposes, a forecast is valuable in proportion as it is right in relation to the element of time.

The earlier economic forecasters sought the key to the situation in the science of astronomy. It is hardly fifty years since the mathematical economist, W, Stanley Jevons, developed what was perhaps the first forecasting device based on scientific principles, when he sought to make the variations in the spots in the sun a basis of business prophecies. His theory was that, since he found crop yields in India roughly synchronized with changes in these spots and since these crop yields in turn affected business conditions in Europe, the future of business could be gauged by such planetary observations. The use of astronomical data in a radically revised form is now being urged by Prof. H. L. Moore of Columbia University.

Fantastical as Jevons' scheme may sound, his basic theory remains the backbone of present day forecasting. This theory is that changes in the business world do not take place in a haphazard manner, but

[230]

in an orderly way, just as changes in atmospheric and cloud conditions uniformly cause rain. It is the goal of business prophets to ascertain the sequence of changes in the business world and to measure the movements of those factors which are found invariably to be followed by changes in business prosperity and in security and commodity prices.

At present there is a vogue for forecasting services in the business world. At least 40,000 hardheaded business men pay no less than $100 a year for one of eight chief types of business forecasting services now in active use.

Perhaps the most widely known of the forecasting services, though not necessarily the best, is that of the Babson Statistical Organization, of Wellesley Hills, Mass. Roger Babson, the inventor of the system, uses as a fundamental assumption a law borrowed from physics, that action and reaction are equal. Hence, he concentrates his efforts on determining the duration and extent of a period of expansion and prosperity in business, in order to determine the characteristics of the period of depression which follows. He has developed a barometer based on this assumption, plotting each area of expansion and assuming that this area will equal that of the subsequent depression after allowing for a normal margin of growth which is measured separately and which is known in academic circles as "the secular trend." The items which he includes in measuring the progress of business are immigration, business mortalities, yield of leading crops, commodity prices, foreign money rates, Canadian conditions, new construction, bank clearings, railroad earnings, foreign trade, domestic money rates, and stock market quotations.

The soothsayer of Wellesley Hills does not attempt to forecast the length and intensity of a period of expansion, but restricts himself to predictions of slumps in business. He assumes that security values reach their high and low points in the first part of the areas of expansion and contraction. Babson, it seems, does not make his predictions so much upon the basis of the sequence of economic events as upon the assumption that reaction approximately equals expansion when exactly measured. In this respect his barometer is unique. It rests upon an assumption which has yet to be proved to the satisfaction of the great body of economists. Moreover, Babson's system involves the difficulty of determining precisely the line of normal growth (secular trend) which must be allowed for determining the size and character of a business boom.

The Brookmire Economic Service, published in New York City, has a wide appeal among speculators, many of whom are impressed with its value. Its forecasting is based on the premise that stock and commodity prices turn after a change in the trend of a number of business factors which it plots as a composite line. On its guard against minor and irrelevant fluctuations, it provides that the turn of the graph must proceed a certain distance before it is plotted as a major change in the business cycle. Brookmire assumes that a change takes place in the stock prices one month after the change in the business barometer, and in commodity prices, six to seven months thereafter. Therefore should the system prove correct in practice, it gives the business man and security trader sufficient time in which to prepare for the changes forecast.

The following factors are used in making the graph:

1. Speculative activity—an average of forty stocks
2. Domestic production and marketing
3. Ratio of imports to exports
4. Speed of turnover of bank deposits
5. Commercial paper rates
6. Open money market rate in London.

Numbers 2 and 3 of these factors are used because they reflect the stocks of goods in the country in relation to demand. The others indicate sentiment in the country and the status of the money market. The assumption is made that a prolonged depression does not occur when the supply of money is abundant. The present Brookmire system has not been tried over a sufficiently long period of years to permit too broad a generalization as to its value. Its supporters assert that it has proved accurate to date, although it did not give an unmistakable indication of the slump in business that occurred in the fall of 1923 and the spring of 1924 because of the abnormal condition of the money market, the great ease in which prevented the barometer from turning downward. The theoretical basis of this forecasting system coincides with current economic dogma, but the barometer must be appraised by the results it attains.

A third significant barometer of business of very great academic importance and of some practical business value is that of the Harvard Economic Service which adheres to the theory of the business cycle and seeks to determine when a change in the cycle will occur through a study of speculation, business activity, and bank and money conditions. In accordance with changes in these factors, predictions are made as to when we enter a period of depression, which is followed by periods of revival, business prosperity, financial strain, and liquidation of securities, industrial crises, and finally liquidation of commodities. Professor Warren M. Persons, editor of

[234]

the Service, declares that since its inception in 1919 the Harvard system has accurately foretold changes in business conditions and security prices except in 1923, when low money rates offset the reduction in the other items of the index.

Another business barometer is that of the Business Barometer Dial, also published in New York. This device uses a clock on which are shown twelve basic factors grouped as indices of general confidence, business conditions, and general conditions. A study of these factors singly and together is made to determine forecasts.

The Standard Statistics Company, Inc., of New York publishes the Standard Daily Trade Service, in which conclusions are based on general research rather than on any single statistical device. The company, for example, specifically disavows that its index of credit supply alone tells the story of the business and financial future. In this statistical device, the supply of money is carefully charted, and curves representing changes in stock prices and general business are drawn and are shown to lag behind the supply of money curve. This chart is built on the theory that the supply of money is a determining factor in the business cycle, a theory advanced by Professor Irving Fisher, of Yale University, in his exposition of a modification of the quantity theory

[235]

of money. [1] The wholly abnormal character of the money market, at present, resulting from the colossal and unprecedented influx of gold from all parts of the world, is placing a severe test on the universality of this theory of business cycles.

Recognizing this, the Standard Statistics Company freely grants that its index has limitations. Its assertion is that "the curve operates almost infallibly as a forecaster of stock market movements, *under certain conditions.* It forecasts a long downward swing of stock prices, when, coincident with the development of an acute credit strain, it crosses the normal line in a downward direct, thus signaling that the credit supply has been exhausted and there are no longer credit facilities to finance further stock market inflation.

"But there are any number of intermediate downward movements (such as occurred in November 1922; March to August 1923 and February to May 1924) on which the money supply index will give no signal at all. It couldn't, because such movements are entirely independent of credit supply—are caused by other economic factors. The most that can be said of the credit influence on such movements is that a plentiful supply of credit prevents them from developing into major crises—such as was precipitated in the stock market in November 1919."

[1] See Chapter XXXI: On the Alleged Root of All Evil.

Soothsayers in Wall Street

The Standard regards the money index as only one of a hundred tools, it explains. In its service, the Standard studies the outlook in a different industry each day and collects a vast array of significant facts which are interpreted by competent economists and articulated clearly by trained journalists. It is more closely related to the special facts of particular industries than the Harvard Service, for example, and in a sense competes with the trade newspapers as well as with forecasting agencies.

Two other business forecasting services published in New York are those of Moody's Investment Service, and the Poor Publishing Co. The Moody system presents a composite graph similar to those already discussed in connection with its monthly analysis of conditions, but it bases its view of the future on no special theory or particular device. The Poor service goes even further in skepticism as to the validity of statistical devices, denying that barometers can be made effective and restricting itself to general discussion of the more important long term movements of the security market and business.

The American Institute of Finance, of Boston, adheres to the belief that "the only scientific method of forecasting stock market movements and business trend is hard thinking, backed by experience in the intelligent study and interpretation of statistics and

[237]

news as well as human nature." It is not wedded to any system or chart, but does not condemn the use of graphic devices. Besides its weekly bulletin, the Institute offers subscribers a course in speculation and investment. The urge for hard thinking is admirable, but it has not yet been demonstrated that this can be done successfully entirely outside of the head of the operator himself.

Irrespective of the assertions of sales managers, it is the consensus of scientific economists that forecasting is still in an experimental stage and that no perfect instrument of measuring the future has yet been devised. The man who uses a forecasting service in connection with his business or stock market operations should familiarize himself with the method employed and should check the conclusions against his own experience and observations.

Of course, if a perfect forecasting device which was universally accepted were invented, it would soon tend to defeat its own purpose by causing the condition forecast to be brought about immediately. For example, if it should predict that stock prices would rise during the next two months its faithful followers would immediately act on the suggestion and the rise would occur forthwith, and perhaps a severe reaction would take place before the end of two months, instead of the predicted sustained rally.

Soothsayers in Wall Street

The influence of statistical organizations on business is steadily growing. To the force of these services mentioned must be added the effect of information about current and prospective movements in trade disseminated by the daily press, by the steadily improving bulletins of the United States Department of Commerce, and the publications of other governmental bodies, the Federal Reserve Board, and the affiliated Federal Reserve Banks. Dependable information about business is becoming more and more widespread and is perhaps having the effect of lessening the swings in business and finance. Competition in the trade and financial markets is becoming less a matter of information and more a clash of judgment.

Moody's Investors Service, Poor's Publishing Company, The Fitch Publishing Company, and the Standard Statistics Company undertake to rate securities in accordance with their investment merit and marketability. These services are sometimes a convenient check against individual judgment.

The foregoing services all have a value and are in an entirely different category from another type of forecasting which has to do with tips on individual stocks which will rise and fall.

Stock market letter writers in brokerage houses

[239]

.are engaged in a modern specialized adaptation of an archaic art.

Hopefuls who expect to amass tremendous fortunes without mental or physical exertion are perpetually buoyed up by the delusion that if they could read between the lines they would find the key to the solution of the mysteries of the market.

The plain fact is that the writers of market letters have no special pipelines to the divinities who shape the market's ends except where outright pool manipulation is involved. In practice these disseminators of speculative wisdom are sometimes privy to the schemes of those who apply the pulmotor to security prices or to a piece of valuable information imparted by an insider in the affairs of a corporation.

Yet most tips are likely to be misleading. Following them blindly is virtually a certain road to financial ruin.

But even those relatively few tips which are based on real knowledge are of doubtful utility. They constitute only one way guides. They merely say: "Take a market position," but give no time-table instructing the disciples when to change their commitments. The whole theory of pool manipulation on the bull side is to buy stocks cheaply, possibly in an atmosphere beclouded by the circulation of adverse rumors, and then to sell dear, helped by the spreading of favorable reports. Thus those who buy on tips are likely to acquire securities while distribution goes on and hold the bag as quotations fall.

So-called inside information is frequently circulated for manipulative purposes. The astute outsider will therefore be critical toward it, examining the source and checking it in so far as is feasible.

At bottom speculation as now carried on is an individual, not a social, art. To succeed in this engaging fluid activity—and only the exceptionally qualified minority consistently succeeds—the operator must rely primarily on his own judgment, his own reading of the financial signposts and his own capacity to think quickly and to act instantaneously.

The idea that the road to easy fortune lies in slavishly following the dopesters is fallacious. Forecasters, statisticians, and letter writers may contribute useful clues, suggestions and diagnoses, but the speculator who acts on them without transforming such data in the chemistry of his own mentality to conform to his own peculiar requirements is in a fair way to part with his money.

The principal banks and investment houses are perpetually creating a vast array of printed matter on investments which is frequently of real educational value and practical utility.

Still another kind of forecasting fascinates the fringe of the finance district.

Wall Street strives to take the mystery out of to-morrow.

Quoting betting odds on elections and prize fights constitutes an activity outside the legitimate function of financial districts, in my opinion. How accurate are these odds as a forecast of future events? An investigation recently undertaken indicates that such odds are far from infallible. The future obstinately remains unknowable. The citizen with a thirst for knowledge, though he has read the Wall Street odds, must still wait for the event to be certain of the outcome. Political odds, however, seem to be more dependable than sporting odds. If the betters knew nothing about prospects and merely guessed, mathematical laws of chance ought to make them right half the time. The value of their forecasts therefore must be judged by their achievements in excess of a 50 per cent record for accuracy.

The Wall Street betting odds on elections had better than a guessing record, but on world's series and prize fights, blind guesses would have been more accurate.

In the last ten elections, the late odds correctly

forecast the event eight times out of ten. The odds were wrong in 1916 when the late President Wilson beat Charles E. Hughes in an exceedingly close contest, and again in 1918 when Governor Smith defeated former Governor Whitman in New York.

In the case of world's series for baseball championships, the late odds foretold the outcome truthfully only three times out of ten.

As for prize fights, odds on the ten most important events in the squared ring since 1897, correctly forecast the event only four times. Moreover, another study revealed that in nine instances where the championship title changed hands—five in the heavyweight and four in the lightweight class—the odds were wrong in every instance but one. Such are examples of cases of real doubt when the fortune tellers on the outskirts of Wall Street receive their severest test. *The odds show a bad record of performance except in cases where the result was virtually obvious.* These studies, tentative in their character, indicate that man has not yet discovered a formula for robbing Nature of her secrets. The events of the future are still beyond the ken of man. Betting odds and security prices are in this sense little more than average guesses of large numbers of individuals.

CHAPTER XXII

HALF TRUTHS ABOUT WALL STREET AFFAIRS

Delusions and Misconceptions about Finance which Blur the Vision of the Layman.

The law says that, when a stock certificate of the par value of $100 is issued, it shall have back of it assets of the value of $100. To be sure, the law goes on to say that it will not inquire too closely into the actual value of those things which the corporation states to be of the value of $100. Having opened the door so far, the camel, if we may use this metaphor from the arid desert when speaking of watered stock, has thrust his whole body in, till we have certificates "of the par value of $100" that did not represent any assets at all when issued, yet are perfectly law proof. Doubtless, *"of the par value of $100"* does deceive many people.—HASTINGS LYON.

DELUSIONS and legends frequently pervade the financial district and thwart clear thinking without which missteps and losses become inevitable. The most dangerous misconceptions and superstitions are those which rest on a foundation of half truths.

Secure investments can ordinarily be made neither

[244]

on hunches nor tips but on clear thinking or sound advice. The investor whose mind is beclouded with will-of-the-wisp vagaries about finance has within his own consciousness forces at work which are likely to cause the frustration of his aims.

In the primer of the fake stock promoter the delusive analogy looms large. Prospective buyers of shares in a new concern formed to make a foamless soap or non-inflammable gasoline, for example, are keyed to a state of mental excitement by the subtle remark in the prospectus of the promoter that the original investor in the Ford Motor Co., the Bell Telephone Co., the Westinghouse Airbrake and such chain stores as the Great Atlantic and Pacific Tea Co., and the F. W. Woolworth Co., attained fabulous returns on their original investment funds.

The device, on analysis, seems crude and ineffective, yet the fact that its use is a helpful stimulant to the sale of worthless stocks is indicated by its persistent employment.

What are the defects in this type of argument?

In the first place, the success of the Bells, the Westinghouses, and the Woolworths in different fields of activity under unlike conditions, is no indication by any stretch of the imagination that the new promoter will prosper commensurately.

Secondly, if any lesson is to be drawn from the

records of the past, it is scientifically necessary to set up the infinitely larger number of failures against the relatively small number of conspicuous successes.

Thirdly, enterprises that have fared well have almost universally *depended not solely on an idea of their founders' but also on good management.* In referring to the records of the outstanding successes, promoters are seeking to divert the attention of the prospective investor from the paucity of information concerning their own venture. The buyer with an inquiring mind will insist that the security vender eschew generalities about success in the abstract and dwell on the facts concerning his own proposition.

A cognate stunt of the high pressure stock salesman is to hint seductively to the inexperienced, *"Now's your chance to get in on the ground floor."* The inference is that the great profits are realized by those who participate in new promotions from the outset.

The truth is that, taking new propositions by and large, the first stages of their conception and financing are the most hazardous ones and, unless their judgment is extraordinarily discriminating, those who "get in on the ground floor" are more than likely to end up in the basement.

[246]

Half Truths about Wall Street Affairs

The pioneer in most walks of life does necessary and heroic work in pathfinding, but frequently his courage and daring fail to bring him a fortune. In financial propositions, if he has overextended himself, others with less creative imagination but with more acumen, frequently buy in his property under the hammer at a receiver's sale and capitalize the product of the pioneer's boldness and originality.

Even with the fraudulent promotions left out of consideration, the records of business reveal that those with even a good but novel idea must climb an uphill road. The paths to prosperity are more labyrinthine than the simple minded stock salesman indicates.

Let us leave out of consideration the great array of failures. Many enterprises which are at this time among the leaders in their industries paid no dividends on their common stock for many years after incorporation. The American Can Co., for example, a leading maker of cans in this country which was launched in 1901, yielded nothing in dividends to common shareholders until 1922. Thus if a man who had got in on the ground at $3 a share in 1901 held the stock until 1908, he could have sold out at $4 a share. If he held 1000 shares he would have made a profit of $1,000 on a $3,000 investment.

Superficially his gain would seem satisfactory, but if he had placed his funds in securities yielding 6 per cent his return during that period in interest alone would have reached $1,260, or $260 more than he obtained from assuming large risks. If, on the other hand, he held on to the American Can until 1924, when the stock sold as high as 138, he would have been compensated for the lack of financial return for twenty-three years in the appreciation of his principal sum.

Take another outstanding industrial leader. The United States Steel Corporation is the dominant factor in the iron and steel industry. However, the investor who bought the common stock in 1901 when it was first offered was not especially pleased with the fruits of his daring three years later when the shares sold at the open market priced at 8⅜. For the first fourteen years of its existence the company paid an average dividend of 2.70 per cent—less than the surer interest rate paid by the savings bank. The records show that the investor who did not acquire steel shares until about 1915 at about $40 for stock that two years later sold as high as $135 and that paid in the meantime dividends totaling more than 20 per cent on his investment, fared better.

These illustrations reveal the record of the relatively few of tens of thousands of new undertakings that succeeded. Those who are among the initial victims of a failure have nothing to show for the speculation except worthless stock certificates—and perhaps a healthy distrust of stock promoters and peddlers.

The meaning of *par value* has confused many laymen. The most common par value for stock is $100 a share, although other figures, such as $50, are sometimes used. Par value is a fictitious normal which in practice has no relation to the market or intrinsic value of a security.

Par value represents little more than a formal accounting method for capitalizing the hopes and enthusiasms of the promoters.

And yet the unworldly will again and again pick up the financial page of the newspaper and run through the stock quotations, naïvely assuming that those shares which are selling below par are likely to be cheap and those selling above par are expensive. Nothing could be further from the truth. The stock of one company having a par value of $100 and selling at $250 a share might and frequently is a great bargain, whereas that of an emaciated competitor also with a value of $100 selling at $18 might be quoted far above its real worth.

Recently, a number of state legislatures have recognized the adverse effects of misconception about par value and there has been a tendency in New York, Ohio and other states to permit the issuance of no par value stock which pretends to be no more than it really is—a share representing the stockholder's partial equity in the residual assets of the company.

The *"book value"* or net assets applicable to the common stock constitutes a better indication of its intrinsic merit than the par printed on the face of the certificate.

Book value is determined by subtracting from the assets shown in the balance sheet of the company sums equivalent to the amount of bonds and other prior claims outstanding, including net current liabilities, and dividing the result by the number of shares of stock outstanding. Where preferred stock is outstanding assets enough to cover the par value of the preferred stock must be deducted also before attaining the book value of the common stock. It is customary to omit good will and other intangible items in determining book value.

There is a tyranny in print. One type of mind accepts as the gospel truth anything that comes off the presses.

The balance sheet and an income account which are the means by which in accounting terminology

[250]

a corporation reveals its inner self to the world are like newspaper editorials,—statements of opinion. By inflating indefinite items on the balance sheet, such as real estate or machinery, or by placing wholly arbitrary values on good will and other intangible items, a corporation can make itself appear more affluent than it really is. In such systems the book value will have little relation to its true worth.

Demonstrated earning power is often a better clue to the real worth of a share of stock than theoretical book value.

A curious scheme by which brokers frequently prevail upon suckers to come back for more punishment is the theory of averaging. The practice of averaging or adding to one's holdings of a stock that goes down is an outgrowth of the theory that whatever goes down must eventually come back. The investor who averages may, for example, double his ownership of a given stock every time it declines ten points. If the first block was bought at 50 and he took an equal block at 40, then a rise to 45 would permit him to break even on his transaction.

Frequently buying of this kind merely results in throwing good money after bad.

The investor who keeps on buying a steadily deteriorating security as the price sinks gets little satisfaction from having reduced the average price of his holdings when the concern goes into bankruptcy and he is left with an accumulation of valueless engraved certificates.

Averaging is frequently held out as a lure by unscrupulous brokers to induce inexperienced security buyers to increase their speculative commitments. A man without large monetary resources and exceptional financial intelligence should invest (seeking security of principal and assured regularity of income), not speculate (seeking profit through an appreciation of principal). The investor who buys primarily to attain safety does not have to worry about reducing his average cost.

A good working rule is: *never average unless the security on its own merits seems attractive at the lower figure.*

Another practice which is a frequent cause of loss to amateur speculators is the use of the *"stop loss order."* This device entails instructing a broker to sell a security at the market when and if it touches a stipulated quotation, usually several points below the current price. If, for example, the stop loss order is placed at 95 when the stock is selling at 100, it doesn't mean that the customer is certain to get 95, but merely that when the stock touches 95 it

[252]

will be offered for sale at the best price obtainable.

Frequently professional speculators make drives against particular stocks for the very purpose of uncovering stop-loss orders. Thus the stop loss order frequently results in a sacrifice sale of securities at a quotation several points below the price at which they could have been sold before or after this particular speculative onslaught. The stop loss order is a profitable device only when used with discrimination by those familiar with the mechanics of the stock market. A good time to use it is at the crest of a wave of speculation when securities appear to be selling well above their intrinsic value as a result of the mere momentum of the forward movement. The investor in such circumstances can advantageously employ a stop loss order so that he will not be caught when the inevitable turn comes.

Another question which periodically becomes a subject of acrimonious debate is the issue of short selling. *A "short sale" is the sale of a security which one does not own, but which one borrows to fulfill the contract to deliver and which one later hopes to buy at a lower price to repay the individual who lent the stock.*

Amateurs have professed to see immorality in the practice of short selling on the ground that it undermines the credit structure of the nation and interferes with business progress. However, economists who have studied the question have long been of the opinion that short selling is a good rather than an evil, since it tends to bring about greater stabilization in prices than would be the case with everyone trading only on the buying side of the market. Short selling creates a demand for stocks when the rank and file are seeking to sell out on a declining market as the buyers cover their commitments—buying back stocks which they have borrowed. Morever, short selling at times of excessive optimism tends to check unduly high swings above intrinsic value. The risks of short selling are somewhat greater than those of speculation for the rise and as a matter of business prudence the amateur does well to eschew the practice.

It is difficult to reduce speculation to a single formula.

One of the generally accepted maxims along the row where money sprouts is "One can't go broke taking profit."

Profit taking before it is too late is usually a good policy, but this glib precept does not tell the whole story. If the speculator is tempted to sell out for a very narrow profit, he is likely to find that the game is not worth the candle. His apparent narrow gains are likely to be effaced by the overhead cost of speculation, which includes broker's commissions, interest on borrowed money, state and federal transfer taxes, and income imposts.

The trader who is always in and out of the market in quest of one and two point profits is almost certain to make money for his broker but not for himself.

The investor who is really buying income should as a general rule ignore minor swings in market quotations. Ordinarily good investments move up and down as a class and switching from one to another yields little except commissions for the broker.

Another self-evident truism of Wall Street —*"Buy stocks on the dips and sell them on the bulges"*—is unlikely to lead the layman on to fortune.

For in the first place the overhead cost of speculation makes in and out trading on narrow margins likely to be unprofitable for non-members of stock exchanges.

Secondly, what may appear to be a mere temporary dip to the more inexperienced man may be the first drop in a major downward movement which might either efface the margin of a small speculator or compel him to tie up his capital in a speculative commitment many months longer than he had intended.

Thirdly, watching the day-to-day price fluctuation tends to form a speculative habit which is likely to be a costly one for the amateur.

Another seemingly self apparent truth is that *"real estate is always safe, it cannot get away from you."* The fallacy here is in connection with price. Though well selected urban property in the United States tends to appreciate in value as the country develops, it is not true that one can buy a parcel of real estate at any price and be sure of recovering the principal.

Even in New York City neighborhoods shift. While general values may be rising, certain localities depreciate. A real estate operator recently remarked that 90 per cent of the land sold by promoters is worth less four or five years after the promotion of the development scheme than when it was offered as a great bargain. "I have made money buying lots which tired owners would sell for a song or which they were willing to let go rather than pay the taxes," he declared. "Sometimes I have bought land for less than 25 per cent of the price at which the land was offered to the public."

[256]

Half Truths about Wall Street Affairs

Solemn but ill-informed purchasers of first liens on worthless property which existed primarily in the imagination of the promoter have frequently been deluded by the words "gold bond" or "gold note" engraved on the face of the security. In the United States since the passage of the Gold Standard Act of 1900, the holder of any claim to United States currency may legally demand payment in gold.

Consequently the use of the word gold on the bond adds nothing to its security, but merely impresses the unknowing.

In foreign countries, such as Germany, however, obligations are payable in paper money only, unless payment in gold is specifically promised. Since the somersaulting of the German mark toward worthlessness, the question of payment in gold has become extremely important.

In the case of foreign government securities held by Americans, the medium of payment is a matter of genuine significance. Most of the foreign loans floated in New York are specifically payable in United States gold coin. In such cases the foreign buyer assumes the risk of fluctuations in foreign exchange, for in order to get United States gold coin, the foreign governments must employ a varying number of francs, lire, and pounds sterling, as the case may be. Where obligations are payable in

[257]

foreign coin, the American owner must bear the risk of changes in exchange rates in addition to the investment risk.

In inverse ratio to a salesman's integrity he will tend to rush prospective customers into decisions concerning investment matters. The fake stock salesman will urge a prospect to buy now because prices will be higher next week. Such a remark indicates blue-sky methods and may mean merely that the promoter will arbitrarily set a higher price on the stock the following week in order to whet the buying appetite.

Individuals, unfamiliar with the mysteries of the investment market, are misled by the customary announcement by high-grade underwriting houses, a few minutes after the subscription books for a new issue have been opened, that they have been closed and that the issue has been fully subscribed. Such an announcement does not mean that it is too late for the investor to buy a bond, but merely indicates that the underwriting house and its associates have in the capacity of wholesalers distributed the bonds to retailers or bond houses, which, in turn, through their salesmen will undertake secondary distribution of the securities to the final investors who will place them in their safe deposit boxes.

[258]

CHAPTER XXIII

BIG BUSINESS FLIRTS WITH VIRTUE

Significance of the Better Business Movement.

The banker has ceased to be reputable who, satisfied with the creed "Caveat Emptor" (let the buyer beware), washes his hands of his customer after he has unloaded his wares. —George B. Caldwell.

American business is steadily striving to raise its ethical standards. The cynical old sophistry—"business is business"—is much less frequently used as a defense against sharp trade practices. Conversely, progressive attempts have been made to develop Korans of commerce which set up codes of fair dealing. Since 1911, when the Associated Advertising Clubs of the World was formed, legitimate business has had an organized conscience. As an offspring of the Associated Advertising Clubs of the World, thirty-eight Better Business Bureaus have been established throughout the country.

The first bureau was launched in Minneapolis in 1914 with H. J. Kenner, who is now manager of the

Common Sense of Money and Investments

Better Business Bureau of New York as secretary. Since that time a new profession of specialists in detecting abuses in the financial and commercial world has come into being. The Better Business movement started as a result of a voluntary impulse on the part of legitimate enterprise to protect the public from exploitation by misleading advertisers, and to protect itself from unfair competition on the part of the unscrupulous. The Bureaus gradually widened the scope of their activities to include questionable trade practices outside of advertising and later reached the financial and security world. The public can help by quickly reporting experiences with fraudulent venders and can get assistance by making inquiries at the bureaus before dealing with unknown concerns.

The Better Business Bureau of New York, which was started in July, 1922, was organized on the initiative of a group of men who sought to set up an agency to prevent abuses in stock selling. Up to the present time the major service rendered by the bureau, under the intelligent direction of Mr. Kenner, has been in connection with exposing fraudulent and questionable stock selling methods. The bureau was created in a time of emergency, when the small investor was being robbed, on the one hand, by an unscrupulous group of bucketeers, many of whom have since gone into bankruptcy, and on the other, by cohorts of blue-sky promoters who sold worthless stock certificates and hot air at fancy prices.

The bureau is at a point of transition, and is laying plans for widening the scope of its activities. A bulletin recently issued calls attention to the fact that steps are now being taken to organize a merchandise section of the bureau, which will call attention to misleading practices of merchants.

It is to be hoped that the Investors' Section of the bureau will begin to devote more and more attention to improving the standards of Wall Street and to making a scientific study of present day methods. If it is to be a Better Business Bureau in the fullest sense of the word, it ought to strive to heighten the standards of the so-called reputable factor in trade and finance and should not confine its activities exclusively to police work in detecting fraud.

The reactionary, in whatever department of life, believes that ultimate truth has been discovered and that the proper procedure consists in swatting the heads of those who differ with accepted notions. The true progressive, on the other hand, though accepting a body of principles as valid and guiding, recognizes that life is dynamic and subject to change, and that methods of living must be adjusted to conform with changing conditions.

[261]

The men at the helm of the Better Business Bureau have, I believe, this larger ideal of making the good factors in trade and finance better as well as to expose crooks, and their financial supporters should encourage them to seek to raise the moral tone of business.

Better Business Bureaus are extra-legal bodies and, because of their very nature, must continually fight for existence and justify their right to live by good works. They have no place in the community unless their aim is improvement of this public service. They should not be snoopers nor self-appointed censors, but can serve a really useful function in articulating the rising standards of conduct of the better elements in economic life.

CHAPTER XXIV

LESSONS FROM THE LIVES OF FIELD MARSHALS OF INDUSTRY

Mistakes of Success Magazines; not all Rich Men are Heroes; nor are they all Villains.

Our business didn't grow of its own accord. We didn't sit still and do nothing but draw dividends. Our business grew for the same reason that other successful businesses grow: our basic principles were right; we dealt justly with everybody and met our obligations promptly; we studied facts; we watched for opportunities and also created opportunities; we spared no expense and no efforts to manufacture a product of the best grade; we did not short-sightedly curtail our market by charging exorbitant prices but constantly aimed at reducing them to a minimum so as to encourage wider and wider consumption; we allowed neither success nor temporary setbacks to cause us to lose our heads; and always we were careful to keep our financial condition sound and strong, resisting all temptation and all suggestions to put out unwarranted amounts of shares to foster speculation or create inflation.—JOHN D. ROCKEFELLER.

There is no secret about success. Success simply calls for hard work, devotion to your business at all times,

[263]

day or night. I was very poor and my education was limited, but I worked very hard and always sought opportunities.—HENRY C. FRICK.

INFINITE are the roads to paradise and the ways to success.

Frequently men of affairs are at their worst when they seek to give recipes for advancement. They are more likely than not to misjudge what qualities in their own make-up brought success.

One man will attribute his development to punctuality; another to power of concentration; another to the capacity for hard work; still another to inventiveness and originality; and yet another to loyalty and enthusiasm.

All of the foregoing qualities are significant and play a part in a man's life, but they are ordinarily not the uniquely characteristic elements of extraordinary success.

What then is the essential difference between the hundred dollar a day and the five dollar a day man? It is, I think, the difference between a creative individual and a routineer, between a pathfinder and a rut-follower.

The hundred-dollar-a-day man has imagination and gives it free play, whereas the five-dollar-a-day man fears the hazards of independent thinking.

Even though a man may be president of a large

corporation or owner of a great block of securities, he can hardly be called a success if he lacks the attitude of intellectual independence.

Every man, of course, is the judge of his own success. To one, success means composing an enduring tone-poem, to another painting a beautiful portrait, to another the capacity to make a brilliant oration, to another the power and prestige that come from business leadership, and to still another merely the monotonous piling up of a heap of gold.

The success magazines operate under the delusion that all rich men are heroes. Muck-raking magazines of disaffection go to the other extreme by assuming that all men of wealth are enemies of the people and inherently vicious.

At the intersection of Broad and Wall Streets, the financial center of the universe, one finds successful men of a great variety of temperaments. They differ among themselves almost as much as shoemakers, actors, and journalists. Not all of them got to the top by adhering to copy book maxims. Occasionally the divorce court records reveal the more sordid side of lives of some men of affairs, but as a class they are certainly no worse than any group with equal opportunities.

The success magazines are seemingly developed on the theory that, if everyone works diligently enough, 110 million bank presidencies will open up. It is true that America has not yet become stratified and that each month scores of individuals are climbing slowly from poverty to riches. That opportunity to rise from the ranks is one of the characteristic aspects of American business life.

However, though each lowly private in the ranks of industry can *theoretically* become a captain, it is also true that only the *exceptional* individuals in the group rise to the top. The others must be content to follow a leader.

Biography is one of the richest forms of literature and men and women will always find inspiration in the stories of outstanding individuals. However, to serve their purpose the biographer of contemporary successes should present their subjects in true perspective, portraying the faults as well as the virtues. Press-agent versions that suppress all the human frailties and stress only artificial qualities make the leaders of industry and finance appear to the general public less warmly human than they really were.

An outstanding lesson from the lives of men of the forefront of industry is that *the leaders recognize the fluidity of human events.* They know that the final rule has not yet been formulated. They perceive that progress and development still lie ahead to chal-

[266]

lenge their ingenuity. *They know that things as they are, are not as good as they will be.*

The failure is the man who thinks that he would have found useful things to do if he had been born about fifty years earlier.

CHAPTER XXV

THE CUSTOMER BUYS THE PLANT

Consumer Ownership of Public Utilities as an Alternative to Municipal Ownership.

It is hard to make the ordinary depositor in a savings bank, or the holder of a small life-insurance policy, understand that unnecessary, unwise and harmful legislation or political action directed against railroads, public utilities and other business affects his savings. The connection is too remote. The lesson is more easily learned when an individual is personally and directly a stockholder in the business under attack.—THOMAS N. MCCARTER.

CARTOONISTS effectively reflect the ebb and flow of political and economic movements in the United States.

Since the wider distribution of securities which began with the sale of Liberty Bonds, newspaper artists have been less inclined to present the typical bondholder as a bloated figure with a huge black cigar in his mouth and a huge face puffed and flabby from self-indulgence. Similarly there is a slow revolution going on in the attitude of consumers toward public service corporations in American cities. The

[268]

time has not yet come when each customer goes out of his way to express his love and admiration for the gas, electric light or telephone company, but the blind intemperate hatred of public utility enterprises of pre-war times is being tempered by a more sympathetic understanding of the uses and functions of such corporations.

Some one tipped off the public service corporations to the preachings of Karl Marx on the subject of economic determinism. They have learned that, if their customers become owners of their securities also, the consumers are less likely to rail and rant at the public service corporations. Instead of looking across a continent for financial aid, electric light, gas and power companies have found ample sources of capital in their own city among their own patrons.

The magic of the idea of customer ownership of public utility corporations has swept across economic America with startling rapidity in the last five years. It has developed as a singularly American alternative to municipal or state ownership. It is a cross between socialism, on the one hand, and self-seeking individualism, on the other.

Customer ownership is temporarily turning gas fitters, telephone operators and meter readers into stock salesmen. It is a scheme of banker-less finance. Instead of going to a middleman and sell-

[269]

ing securities to him, public utility companies engaged in customer ownership campaigns temporarily transform their own electric light, gas, power, telephone organization into a corps of security-venders.

The gas man, central, and the other employees of the public service concerns in their solicitations reach individuals who never before bought securities and thus bring the gospel of thrift to new places, helping the individual and at the same time tapping additional sources of capital which contribute to the tremendous expansion of the utilities which is now going on in the United States.

The system of customer ownership has thus far been confined to public utility enterprises. It could also, in my opinion, be profitably employed by the railroads. It is, however, not so well adapted to the needs of industrial corporations for they are unregulated industries subject to little check besides that embodied by the sense of honor and responsibility of the management. Public utility enterprises, on the other hand, are under the supervision of state commissions which check up on their security offerings and which compel the publication of authentic periodic records of earnings and expenses by which the changing worth of the securities may be measured.

Of course, all public utility securities are not of

equal worth. Some are excellent, some are fairly good, and some are wholly undesirable. Thus far the consumer ownership movement has been held within reasonable bounds and has related primarily to preferred stocks of sound companies. The Pacific Gas and Electric Co., which was one of the pioneers in this development, has recently widened the scope of the movement by offering for the first time common stock to consumer owners.

Although the bankers are left out of the consumer ownership movement they are no longer hostile to its development. Investment bankers who bring out bond issues of public utility enterprises realize that the value of the bonds is heightened by the sale of junior securities.

Instead of using the arid unappealing traditional type of advertising copy of the old-fashioned conservative bond houses, the public utility companies have sought to speak in a language that the general public will understand. They have translated the mysteries and obscurities of finance into concrete formulas embodying the objectives of thrift. Moreover, having taken a leaf from the United States government which distributed its own obligations with unprecedented thoroughness by permitting individuals of small means to buy securities on the partial payment plan, the utilities in asking their customers to buy their securities permit them to make a small payment down and to pay the balance in regular installments over a period of time, frequently as long as one year. The partial payment scheme, making it possible for the individual to save out of current income in a convenient and automatic manner, is highly desirable. After the Armistice, however, it was exploited by bucketeers who by subtle devices stole the installment payments of their customers. Solid houses with few exceptions were averse to the system because of the added expense in bookkeeping entailed. The individual should avoid opening partial payments with any house to who.. he would not be willing to lend money.

Executives who have fostered the consumer ownership movement assert that it has accomplished three main results. First, it has taught the wider public the fundamentals of sound investment, thus adding stability to communities. Secondly, it has cultivated good will for utilities by enormously widening its circle of interested friends. Thirdly, it has provided a significant new source of capital.

The political factor is especially important. The welfare of regular public utility concerns depends to a large extent to the attitude of the public toward it. A hostile public often makes constructive regu-

[272]

lation by commissions difficult if not impossible. Moreover, a friendly public renders discriminatory legislation less popular. Thus when the public utility company sells stocks to a wide number of its own customers, it automatically increases the safety of the security offered, for the antipathy of the public is one of the major risks involved in an investment of this kind and this feeling of hostility has been found to wane when owner- ship of the company's stock becomes widespread in the community. It was this aspect of the question which gave the public ownership plan its greatest stimulus, especially during the post-war period when public utility credit was severely strained and public opposition was strong.

Electric companies which are among the strongest financially have been pioneers in this work.

One selling device is to urge the use of the divi- dends on stocks bought to pay for service rendered by the company.

The American Telephone and Telegraph Company, the holding company for subsidiary Bell Telephone Companies throughout the country, which employed this argument, *now has more than 300,000 share- holders, more than any other business enterprise in the world.*

[273]

The subjoined table indicates the growth of the consumer ownership movement.

Year	Shares Sold	Stockholders Obtained
1914	92,310	4,044
1915	57,103	4,357
1916	38,057	3,681
1917	79,348	7,470
1918	30,783	4,115
1919	166,096	20,840
1920	416,089	62,885
1921	802,845	118,177
1922	1,750,707	198,018

Electric light companies affiliated with the National Electric Light Association sold directly to the customers, $80,000,000 of securities in the fiscal year ended June 30, 1922; $175,000,000 in the year ended June 30, 1923, and more than $300,000,000 in the year ended June 30, 1924. In 1920 this group sold only $35,000,000 of securities.

One of the great needs at the present time is to set up standards for the consumer ownership movement to prevent weaker companies on the verge of receivership from luring customers into highly speculative securities. Self-interest, however, acts somewhat as a deterrent so that it is unwise and unprofitable for an individual company or companies in gen-

[274]

eral who aim primarily to win public esteem and friendship, to foist questionable or undesirable securities on the general public. However, in buying junior securities the public is necessarily assuming business risks and should keep in touch with the earning power of companies in which it has invested.

Moreover, a ready open market should be made either by the companies themselves, or even better, on stock exchanges for such securities. Liquidity or ability to turn securities into cash is a desirable investment attribute. Furthermore an individual ought to be able to free himself of an investment commitment when and if he perceived that the economic trend is unfavorable.

In some cities an effort is being made to give customers who have acquired securities a real sense of ownership in the properties. Committees of customer owners have been organized and have been invited to make suggestions as to improvement of service and to advise on expansion programs. Where properly supervised, the customer ownership movement is psychologically and financially sound for it is based on human longings for coöperation and good service and places self-interest of a large element in the community behind the well-being of public service enterprises.

[275]

CHAPTER XXVI

BANKS FOR THE IMPECUNIOUS

Loan Sharks versus Coöperative Lenders.

When seventy thousand Americans with next-to-no capital can in ten years and in fifteen states build, operate, and completely control over two hundred credit unions, or baby banks, with combined assets of more than twelve millions, most of which is safely and beneficially loaned out among themselves in amounts of from five to two thousand dollars, what's the answer?

Certainly, that the United States needs low-cost, small-loans service.—GERTRUDE MATHEWS SHELBY.

EXPLOITING poverty has long been a profitable pursuit for loan sharks, unregulated pawn brokers, and loan societies which in some states charge up to thirty-six per cent interest to needy borrowers.

Frequently, a man of character but no funds can obtain accomodation on far more advantageous terms from service organizations which were created primarily to help him but which, because of their less aggressive sales methods, do not become known to him.

There are many types of financial institutions

which touch the average man in his daily life and of which relatively little is heard. The more familiar institutions of the masses—the great mutual savings banks, life insurance companies, and savings and loan associations—operate efficiently and safely, and therefore remain outside the company of those who get on the front pages of the newspapers.

Since 1910, and particularly during the last four years, there has been in this country a striking growth of poor man's banks, which take two forms, First, the coöperative National and state banks, of which the Brotherhood of Locomotive Engineers' Co-operative National Bank of Cleveland is the model; secondly, credit unions, which are banks in miniature.

Credit unions are less formal organizations, whose unique character consists of exceedingly small operating expenses. A desk and a set of books are frequently the only equipment required. Often the officers of credit unions volunteer their services and get free desk room.

Credit unions undertake to finance the poor. They extend credit to individuals of good character who would be unable to get accomodations at ordinary banks, either because the amount involved would be too small, or because they were without resources which could be used as security for a loan.

Credit unions represent a revolt against the tend-
[277]

ency of ordinary commercial banks to require minimum deposits, such as $200.

The ordinary credit unions admit as members those
who pay an entrance fee of 25 cents and as little as
10 cents a share weekly on the instalment plan. Besides, deposits in small amounts are accepted. They
operate under state supervision.

The funds secured from the sale of membership
shares and from deposits are used as the basis of
loans to needy members. At times, when demands
from members do not absorb all the available funds,
the excess can be used to purchase Government bonds,
bank acceptances and commercial paper, which are
highly liquid bank investments.

The theory behind the credit union is that, though
the individual wage-earner, standing alone, is a weak
figure in the cold world of give and take, when he
bands together with several hundred others the union
of meager financial resources becomes a powerful
weapon for keeping the wolf away.

Credit unions have the capacity to transform a
member's good character into a negotiable instrument which will pay rent during illness, or buy medicine or food. Credit unions have been organized in
governmental departments, among the employees of
corporations, in churches, lodges and in farming
communities.

[278]

Banks for the Impecunious

Roy F. Bergengren, in his book on credit unions called "Coöperative Banking," recites some typical situations: A loan from a credit union enabled a widow to set up in business as a public stenographer, financed a war veteran who went into the junk business, provided for a tubercular cure and furnished the means for taking care of pressing loans arranged on usurious terms.

Since the aim of credit unions is service to members, rather than profits to shareholders, persistent effort has been made to keep interest rates on loans as low as feasible. Despite this policy, the better managed credit unions have grown rapidly and have earned substantial profits.

Massachusetts was the first of the States to authorize the credit unions. Starting in 1915, New York credit unions are now larger in both assets and total membership than the Massachusetts institutions. The latest available report indicates eighty-two credit unions with total assets of $4,445,297, and among their members are included 18,752 borrowers and 14,728 non-borrowers. There are now 100 credit unions in the state and 240 throughout the country.

CHAPTER XXVII

"ONE DOLLAR DOWN AND ——"

Advantages and Hazards of the Rapidly Developing use of the Installment Plan.

It is an open question whether or not the installment method is an unmixed blessing to the public. On one side is the theory that the plan has brought within the reach of the small wage earner many of the refinements and luxuries of life, thereby raising the standard of living in the American home. Opposed to this is the contention that "easy payments" operate to lead improvident people into expenditures and debt unjustified by their incomes and station in society.—R. S. WHITE.

THE American people are going more and more into debt for their automobiles, furniture, jewelry and even clothing.

The tendency to buy now and pledge a share of next year's income has brought criticism from austere banking quarters. Yet the habit seemingly grows, and plays an important part in keeping consumption on an exceedingly high basis.

The standard of living in this country is at present

about as high as it has ever been. For the average family, the luxuries of the last generation have become the necessities to-day. Wants have multiplied, and the common run of men have sought in increasing ways to gratify the desires of their families.

The democratization of material comforts is certainly a thing to be desired. In so far as the installment system has contributed to the better standard of living, it has had beneficial aspects. And yet the question remains whether financing consumption on a large scale is safe banking and sound policy.

No general answer can be given to these inquiries, for the desirability of the system depends on the degree to which it is used. For their own self protection, merchants should exercise scrupulous care to avoid overloading their customers with obligations.

The ordinary commercial bank, whose first duty is to keep safe the funds of depositors which have been entrusted, is rightly disinclined to finance consumption. Hence new agencies have been developed for this purpose.

Naturally regular banks prefer to finance production, which is a wealth creating process intended to yield funds with which to pay off the loan. Good bank loans should be self-liquidating. Such loans are regularly made by banks to manufacturers to finance them between the time the raw material is purchased and the finished goods sold and paid for.

Consumption goods, such as clothing, are not income producing. Presumably they yield sufficient pleasures to justify the buyer in obligating himself to pay for them. But payments depend not upon the wealth creating capacity of the clothing or jewelry bought on the installment plan, but upon the earning power of the buyer.

As long as relatively prosperous times exist and labor is rather fully employed at high effective wages, this system of mortgaging the next few months' pay envelopes works smoothly. Widespread unemployment or wage reductions would tend to throw sand into the credit machinery, and would cause the installment houses and finance companies to repossess the articles of consumption at a time of slackened demand for such merchandise. Loans based upon such operations would tend to become frozen and might have to be radically written down.

In so far as the individual is concerned, these rules tend to suggest wise procedure:

First: never buy consumption goods on the partial payment plan if you are able to pay cash, for the credit substitute is expensive and the cost falls on the buyer.

Second: limit installment purchases to commodi-

[282]

"One Dollar Down and—"

ties of an essential character whose benefits will extend at least over the entire period of payment. For example, it would be uneconomic to buy theater tickets on the installment plan, but it would be justifiable to buy permanent things such as a house or even a piano on this basis.

Third: if necessary to buy on the installment plan, play safe and figure on adverse contingencies, such as loss of time which would reduce your income. In other words, don't mortgage your current and prospective income up to the hilt except for emergencies, such as illness and operations, but leave an ample margin.

Living well depends not only on the size of a family's income, but also on the astuteness with which it is spent. Sometimes ease of payment on the installment plan leads to extravagant and less essential purchases.

On the other hand, there is nothing intrinsically and necessarily unsound upon the partial payment plan when used to finance the purchase of permanent or semi-permanent things.

Without credit, home buying on a large scale would be impossible.

Without credit, the sale of automobiles on the present scale would be utterly beyond accomplishment.

[283]

Henry Ford remarked, in this connection, that where the people desire a thing intensely enough they can find a way to pay for it.

Buying securities on the partial payment plan is in a somewhat different category. It is universally desirable where the financial house is thoroughly dependent and the securities bought of a high investment character. The habit started with borrowing to buy Liberty bonds. Later bucketshops capitalized these new tendencies, and mulcted many individuals.

Where good securities are purchased from reputable houses, the buyer, in case of inability to meet future payments, can protect his equity through ordering the readily marketable securities sold.

CHAPTER XXVIII

AVOIDING BANKRUPTCY IN THE PANTRY

Budgeting: The Problem of Intelligent and Systematic Spending.

The great street car systems of the country get their power from central stations, direct from generators, but they are also storing in batteries a sufficient quantity of current so that when the producing machinery is incapacitated for a season there will be something to draw on so that the wire may at all times be kept alive and the cars moving. Get a battery for yourself, in the shape of a bank account, and see that day by day something is stored up for the time when either your producing mechanism may be incapacitated or be worn beyond repair.—HENRY FORD.

SYSTEMATIC spending by means of a budget means buying in accordance with a well conceived policy rather than yielding ineffectually to the miscellaneous appeals of a thousand and one business men who have something to sell.

Just as the story of success or failure of a business corporation lies with management, so the well

[285]

being of a family depends not only on the income of the bread winner but also largely on the managerial skill of the mother who runs the household.

Every executive deducts something from the sum total of purchasing power of the family and the astute individual will not relinquish power except in return for valuable and satisfying things. Food, shelter and clothing come first and all other considerations must yield to them. Operating expenses, development, and culture, and saving, and reserves also deserve consideration in every man's budget.

A dependable index of an individual's well being is not his gross income alone but really his net income, *namely that which is saved at the end of the year after paying living expenses.*

Expenditures for rent, food and clothing are more or less fixed and make insistent claims on the individual's income. Other forms of expenditure, involving small but frequent outlays for sundry extravagances and satisfaction of temporary whims have a tendency gradually to expand and encroach on funds reserved for saving.

Therefore, unless the individual has a will of iron or some automatic scheme of investment such as a contract for the purchase of shares in a building and loan association, the purchasing of high grade securities on the partial payment plan, or endowment insurance, he is likely to find at the end of the month that sundry unexpected spendings exhausted his allotment for thrift purposes.

Differing tastes and living standards make it impracticable to formulate universally acceptable budgets. One family will prefer to economize on rent in order to have additional reserves for the education of their children. Another will cut down on clothing in order to enjoy the luxury of the opera. Still another most unwisely will cut down on food expenditures in order to bedeck themselves with gay and attractive clothing.

Moreover, the factor of rent varies from community to community. It must necessarily constitute a larger proportion of total expenditures in the large cities where tens of thousands are competing with one another for a given foot of space.

Ready made budgets therefore are likely to be of little value to a family except as suggestions by means of which they are helped to construct their own budget which best expresses their aspirations, geared to their own financial resources.

Aristotle's golden mean should be followed in budgets as in everything else. *Excessive thrift is as bad as improvidence, for it means saving everything for a to-morrow which will never come.* The savings

[287]

bank section of the American Bankers Association, in presenting the three subjoined typical budgets, reveals this hazard in a picturesque manner.

	Parsimonious Man	Thrifty Man	Extravagant Man
Saves	60%	20%	0%
Living expenses	37%	50%	58%
Education	1%	10%	1%
Recreation	1%	10%	40%
Charity	1%	10%	1%
	100%	100%	100%

The chart headed "Table of Typical Budgets for the American Family" which has been especially prepared for this chapter will help families of varying incomes decide how much should be allotted for various essential purposes. It is based on the average experience of American families.

[288]

TABLE OF TYPICAL BUDGETS FOR THE AMERICAN FAMILY

INCOME		NECESSARY EXPENSES					CULTURAL EXPENSE				SURPLUS	
Annual	Monthly	Food	Shelter	Clothing	Operating expense	% of income	Education and recreation	% of income	Miscellaneous	Insurance	Saving	% of income
$1,500	$125.	$34.	$30.	$22.	$16.	81.7	$10.	8.	$3.	$7.	$3.	10.3
2,000	166.66	42.	40.	26.	23.	78.7	15.	9.	5.	9.	6.66	12.3
2,500	208.33	50.	45.	33.	30.	75.1	22.33	10.7	7.	10.	10.	14.2
3,000	250.	60.	50.	40.	35.	74.	30.	12.	10.	12.	13.	14.
3,500	291.67	65.	60.	45.	40.	72.	36.67	12.6	12.	14.	19.	15.4
4,000	333.33	70.	65.	50.	45.	69.	48.33	14.5	14.	16.	25.	16.5
4,500	375.	72.	70.	60.	50.	67.2	54.	14.4	15.	18.	36.	18.4
5,000	416.67	75.	75.	60.	65.	66.	61.	14.6	18.	20.	42.67	19.4
6,000	500.	85.	90.	70.	75.	64.	75.	15.	22.	22.	61.	21.
7,000	583.33	95.	100.	75.	75.	59.2	100.	17.2	25.	24.	89.33	23.72
8,000	666.66	105.	110.	85.	80.	57.	115.	17.3	30.	28.	113.66	25.7
9,000	750.	110.	120.	90.	100.	56.	132.	17.6	33.	32.	133.	26.4
10,000	833.33	115.	130.	95.	110.	54.	145.	17.4	36.	35.	167.33	28.6
12,500	1,041.67	125.	140.	100.	125.	47.	176.67	17.	40.	40.	295.	36.
15,000	1,250.	130.	145.	110.	130.	41.2	215.	17.2	42.	45.	433.	41.6
20,000	1,666.67	150.	160.	125.	150.	35.1	275.	16.5	45.	55.	706.67	48.4
30,000	2,500.	200.	250.	150.	200.	32.	400.	16.	60.	75.	1,165.00	52.

Note.—This budget table is intended for a family of two adults and two children.

CHAPTER XXIX

PICKING YOUR EMPLOYER AND YOUR JOB

The Problem of Earning; Science of Vocational Guidance.

It is apparent that the old-time concept of personnel work as "putting square pegs into square holes" is entirely inadequate. There is no recognition here of the fact that men and jobs are changing in themselves, and plastic, yielding here and giving there to outside pressure.— WALTER D. SCOTT AND ROBERT C. CLOTHIER.

Since not every kind of work can be done equally well by any individual, misfits in vocation are constantly occurring. Unless great care is exercised, the employees in large commercial and industrial concerns may easily become a shifting population, abandoning their work for loss of interest in it or being dismissed for unsatisfactory service.

"Impressionistic interviews, photographic analysis, letters of recommendation, letters of application and application forms, phrenological and physiognomic descriptions, and numerous other diagnostic aids have in turn been tried and found to be either utterly absurd or manifestly inadequate to determine either general or specific fitness."—H. L. HOLLINGWORTH AND A. T. POFFENBERGER.

Regarding letters of recommendation:
Experienced officials pay but scanty attention to testimonials and letters of recommendation. Americans are apt to be too charitable and good-natured when writing letters of recommendation.—CHARLES W. ELIOT.

IN this land of promise—some of which is fulfilled—we have strayed far from the oriental caste system. Instead of following the beaten path of his father, the modern son, bent on self expression, is more than likely to be tempted to some vocation new to his family. Fathers, thinking of the hardships of their daily grind, assume that the obstacles are peculiar to their profession instead of common to all efforts to earn a livelihood, and frequently advise their offspring to try something different.

The milkman complains of the hardship of rising at three A. M.

The veteran actor deplores night work.

The old time reporter sighs that a lifetime of effort has brought him nowhere.

The banker confesses, that if he is strict with would-be borrowers, they call him a tight-wad, and, if he is lax, his stockholders and depositors call him unsound.

[291]

The farmer regrets his isolation.

When the son followed the footsteps of his father the accident of his birth determined the course of a career. Now that the son has freed himself from the restrictions of family tradition, other accidental factors help to shape the course of his life work.

The mere chance of a want-ad appearing on the day when a boy first thinks of seeking a job, the random offer of an acquaintance, the circumstance of filling in temporarily for a person who is ill or a temporary job taken during vacation, frequently tie an individual to a line of business for the rest of his life.

The selection of professions is frequently equally unscientific. At the age of six a boy will decide that he wants to be a lawyer because his favorite uncle is, or a physician or architect or engineer or teacher or minister, as the case may be.

With the enormously quickened development of psychology in the last few decades we are just beginning to apply scientific methods of adjusting the individual to work for which he is best fitted. The science of keeping square pegs out of round holes is in a developmental stage, but it has not yet actively influenced the choice of the great majority of people.

Intelligent employers are recognizing the value of vocational guidance and are themselves seeking to

[292]

help place men and women at work where they can best utilize their capacities.

Furthermore, development in the direction of tests to determine fitness for special types of work has been made necessary by increased specialization of industry. The war gave great stimulus to these psychological examinations which were generally used to determine the qualifications of recruits. The technique of these examinations has not yet, however, passed the experimental stage, and action based on them should be tempered with common sense. They are at present only suggestive.

"In recent years, the interest in the development of mental tests and scales primarily for the determination of general intelligence or for particular school abilities," H. L. Hollingworth and A. T. Poffenberger point out in their "Applied Psychology," "has led to the hope that in addition to such value as these intelligence and product scales obviously have in vocational selection, specific tests might be devised which would measure such particular aptitudes as might be demanded by a given type of work. If tests could be provided which would enable the employer to select, from a list of applicants, those most likely to be successful at the work in question, this would greatly decrease the loss which all the other aids to selection seem unable to reduce. Even sets

[293]

of tests which would be inadequate for the vocational diagnosis and guidance of the individual might still be of inestimable use to the employer."

The shifting of workers from job to job places a heavy charge on industry. Labor turnover is expensive and indicates inefficient management. The Russell Sage Foundation, in studying this subject, found that a mining company that employed 1,000 men had to hire 5,000 annually, and that a machine shop with 10,000 workers engaged 21,000 workers annually. It is estimated that where the turnover takes place every six months the cost of turnover and training of workers is 20 per cent of the total payroll.

To reduce turnover some concerns have adopted the system of transferring employees who prove ineffectual in one job to another type of work. In the case of the Ford Motor Company, a foreman may discharge a worker only from his own department. Then the central employment office places him in another department where he gets another chance to prove his worth. A similar system is used in the progressive Boston department store of William Filene's Sons.

The schools of the country should give more attention to vocational guidance. To graduating classes lectures on the opportunities and problems of various

[294]

trades and professions should be given. Moreover, it would be helpful if each school, especially in the larger cities, could have on the faculty one instructor trained in vocational psychology, who could be qualified to advise each student as to his own apparent fitness for various types of work.

Of course, no inelastic formula could be evolved to take all the risk and adventure out of career building and, if it could, it would make the whole task of setting out upon one's life work less appealing. However, the advice of intelligent trained teachers could obviate many of the greater maladjustments which make for individual unhappiness and industrial inefficiency.

It is tragic to make a fourth rate baritone out of a first class plumber, or a inept writer out of a potentially good bricklayer, or, on the other hand, to make a ribbon salesman out of a potentially brilliant engineer or surgeon.

In choosing a vocation, the first consideration should be the fitness and personal tastes of the individual concerned. There may be no precise correlation between love of a particular kind of work and one's fitness for it, but other things being equal, the man who can sing while he toils is more likely to succeed or at least be happy.

Work, either humble or otherwise, should give

[295]

the individual opportunity for self-expression. It should, if possible, interest him and call forth his best energies.

Boys and girls, leaving schools, should not trip lightly and thoughtlessly into the first job that becomes available. They should look upon their first place, no matter how unimportant it seems, as the starting point of their career and should analyze thoughtfully their own qualifications for the work contemplated and the logical paths of advancement open if merit is demonstrated.

The contents of the first week's pay envelope are infinitely less important than the paths which lead onward from the first job. If the place leads to a blind alley, it is unattractive for a beginner no matter what the emolument happens to be.

The employer asks for references and scrutinizes each applicant with great care. Young Americans starting out upon their business careers should delicately and diplomatically, but none the less thoroughly, investigate their prospective employer, learning of his attitude toward labor and policy of promotions and willingness to help ambitious youngsters to advance. It is well also to know whether he pays at least the market rate for services rendered, whether he picks executives from the ranks and whether he offers opportunities for study and

[296]

self advancement while one is working. The policy of an employer toward profit sharing and participation of workers in the actual government of the business are further factors to consider.

The most serious problem of the Young American is to start right in his business or professional career. He should take his first job after due deliberation rather than drift blindly into the first opening he perceives. He should not hesitate to ask freely for advice from his teachers and from his friends, nor to write to successful men in the field which he contemplates entering. Many of them would be glad to set a youngster right.

Then too, a youngster should be experimental in his attitude toward his job. If he finds that his first judgment was wrong, he should be quick to revise it and try something else. Many a failure in one type of work has found it possible to do conspicuously able things in another, but the individual who drifts with the economic tides, irrespective of his own will, is unfair to himself. He will carry all the burdens of industry with few of the rewards that come to the individual who tries to be the master of his own fate.

CHAPTER XXX

HOW TO TURN OLD AGE FROM A DEFEAT INTO A TRIUMPH

Financing Retirement; Stepping aside for Younger Men; Permanent Dollar a Year Men.

I am more of a farmer than I am a steel manufacturer, still I keep my hand on the pulse of the old machine as she goes bounding along, and when the boys get in a little trouble sometimes, where they need a little diplomacy, then I step in and help them out, but generally I look on it from a broad point of view. Now, my days of business and industrial activity must necessarily be nearly ended, because it is the day of young men. Young men must progress, young men must go ahead, young men must be happy to be employed.—CHARLES M. SCHWAB.

If we follow Bernard Shaw's suggestion and go "back to Methuselah," the problem of growing old gracefully will be radically altered.

Prosperous individuals as a group have not been entirely successful in the manner in which they attain old age.

[298]

From Defeat to Triumph in Old Age

Some men make the mistake of stepping suddenly out of an office of endless routine and effort into a playground devoid of all obligations. The transition is too swift and frequently causes mental and physical harm. On the other hand, there are those who never are ready to get through with the ordinary responsibilities of business. They refuse to get out of a harness that they have outgrown. They are unready to retire until death calls them.

The newer tendency, however, among successful business men of the first rank is gradually to divest themselves of responsibilities and obligations as they reach the evening of their careers.

Charles M. Schwab believes every individual reaches a stage in his business career when it is wise to step aside and give younger men a chance.

Other business men of a certain temperament are ready to quit their money making activities before it is physically necessary to retire. Moved by a desire to render public service, men of this viewpoint give up their active business careers after they have amassed fortunes and mere money making ceases to hold them as a consuming passion.

During the war, leading business executives closed their desks and went to Washington to serve the government at the nominal salary of one dollar a year. The idea was not dropped with the armistice. There remains a corps of what virtually amounts to permanent dollar a year men—men of the stamp of Frank A. Vanderlip, Bernard M. Baruch, Eugene Meyer, Jr. and Edward Bok.

In the "Americanization of Edward Bok," Mr. Bok, discussing this human problem, says:

. . . "It cannot be denied that the pathetic picture we so often see is found in American business life more frequently than in that of any other land: men unable to let go—not only for their own good, but to give the younger men behind them an opportunity. Not that a man should stop work, for man was born to work, and in work he should find his greatest refreshment. But so often it does not occur to a man in a pivotal position to question the possibility that at sixty or seventy he can keep steadily in touch with a generation whose ideas are controlled by men twenty years younger. Unconsciously he hangs on beyond his greatest usefulness and efficiency; he convinces himself that he is indispensable to his business, while in scores of cases, the business would be distinctly benefited by his retirement and the consequent coming to the front of the younger blood. . . .

"The sad fact is that in all too many instances the average American business man is actually afraid to let go because he realizes that out of business he should not know what to do. For years he has so excluded all other interests that at fifty or sixty or seventy he finds himself a slave to his business, with positively no inner resources. Retirement from the one thing he does know would naturally leave such a man useless to himself and his family and his

[300]

community: worse than useless, as a matter of fact, for he would be a burden to himself, a nuisance to his family, and, when he would begin to write 'letters' to the newspapers, a bore to the community.

"It is significant that a European or English business man rarely reaches middle age devoid of acquaintance with other matters; he always lets the breezes from other worlds of thought blow through his ideas, with the result that when he is ready to retire from business he has other interests to fall back upon. Fortunately it is becoming less uncommon for American men to retire from business and devote themselves to other pursuits; and their number will undoubtedly increase as time goes on and we learn the lessoms of life with a richer background. But one cannot help feeling regretful that the custom is not growing more rapidly.

"A man must unquestionably prepare years ahead for his retirement, not alone financially but mentally as well.

"It is this lesson that the American business man has still to learn: that no man can be wholly efficient in his life, that he is not living a four squared existence, if he concentrates every waking thought on his material affairs. He has still to learn that man cannot live by bread alone. The making of money, the accumulation of material power, is not all there is to living. Life is something more than these, and the man who misses this truth misses the greatest joy and satisfaction that can come into his life—service to others."

Furthermore, there is a new tendency toward semi-retirement among the elder statesmen of business and finance. In the last ten years there has been more

[301]

and more of a disposition of heads of corporations and banks to step out of the presidency and accept the office of chairman of the board of directors, bringing a younger man in as president. The actual relinquishment of power and control varies in each case and depends not only on the by-laws of the particular corporation, but very largely on the personality of the men involved. Ordinarily, as chairman of the board of directors, the older man is available to help formulate the broad policies of an enterprise, but is relieved of the day to day tedium of administering a huge business organization.

To men of conspicuous success, growing old is largely a matter of making one of various choices, but to the average man of relatively small earning power and perhaps no competence, growing old entails serious financial problems.

Since old age is inevitable for all who avoid premature death, financing retirement should be one of the goals of every thrifty individual. While in one's twenties or thirties, one should lay out a plan for building up a retirement fund. It involves *setting up a sinking fund by which earning power is amortized.* Out of each year's current earnings a definite sum should be put aside for old age requirements. Man's physical machine wears out and a thrift fund makes allowance for this constant depreciation.

[302]

From Defeat to Triumph in Old Age

Enough should be put away so that at a given age the income from investments will take care of one's minimum needs. Endowment life insurance, maturing around the age of sixty or sixty-five, is another helpful way of building up an old age fund. One's needs after retirement are smaller than during active life, for no allowance need be made for saving, insurance ór advancement.

The system of pensions involves the recognition of the universal phenomenon of decaying earning power in the latter years of an individual's life. The man or woman who is not eligible for a pension and who prefers at any rate to be an active agent in shaping the course of his own life can over a long period of years easily build up an adequate thrift fund for old age at relatively little sacrifice.

Old age should be a period of great wisdom and reflection. It should be unmarred by worries concerning money matters and by responsibility for the details of business management. It should be an occasion for returning to society and to the younger generations the benefits of accumulated experience.

To be triumphant, old age should be a period of open-mindedness, and accessibility to new ideas, with a consuming desire for unselfish service.

[303]

CHAPTER XXXI

ON THE ALLEGED ROOT OF ALL EVIL

Money: Its Uses and Functions.

It is therefore indispensable that all things which can be exchanged should be capable of comparison, and for this purpose money has come in, and comes to be a kind of medium, for it measures all things and so likewise the excess and defect; for instance, to a house or a given quantity of food.—ARISTOTLE.

EXTREMISTS give expression to the outer ranges of all thought.

There are those on the one hand, who regard money as an instrument of the devil. On the other, equally misguided folk look upon money as God's most favored vehicle of beneficence.

Generalization is a means of intellectual economy and no generalization, including this one, as an astute Frenchman observed, is likely always to be true. Money of itself is neither good nor bad. It is a tool. Its ethical value depends upon its use. As an idol, money is a shrine which is certain to bring disillusionment to those who worship before it. And yet sackcloth and ashes are generally unacceptable to the

[304]

modern generation which perpetually strives to raise its standard of living.

Money is analogous to a man's right arm—nothing to wax poetical or sentimental about but a mighty difficult thing to get along without. The normal individual, appreciating the use of his arm, is not perpetually conscious of its desirability. He takes it for granted and thinks of higher achievements, the accomplishment of which can be facilitated by its use.

Some men, having lost their arm, nevertheless live —sometimes magnificently, but their activities are hampered by the missing member. Likewise some noble souls, absolutely impecunious, radiate happiness and live beautiful, full lives. By and large, however, those without money and right arms are, to say the least, handicapped.

But right arms do not take the place of spiritual values such as the love of a good woman, the devotion of a son, the thrill of a lyric poem, the ecstasy of a symphony, or the companionship of a well-seasoned pipe. And, though a hammer is useful to a carpenter, it does not become the end-all and the be-all of his life.

Academicians tell us that money is a medium of exchange, a standard of value, a store of value, and a standard for deferred payments.

It would be burdensome to exchange pianos directly for bananas. But the piano merchant using dollars and cents as a "medium of exchange" can readily purchase bananas. If primitive barter still prevailed the piano would be priced at 100,000 bananas, for example, but in modern life there is such a multiplicity of commodities that it would be endlessly confusing to express the price in terms of every other commodity. So instead of placing a tag reading "100,000 bananas" on the piano, the merchant expresses the market worth in terms of money—the standard of value.

Money also serves as a measure of the debt of one individual to another. When the produce man sells his customers bananas and other supplies to be paid for at the end of the month, he expects to receive a stipulated number of dollars and cents regardless of what the price of the food stuffs happens to be on the day of payment. As a measure of deferred payments money thus facilitates transactions on a credit basis.

Under ordinary circumstances the safest way to keep fluid wealth is in the form of cash, although this is frequently unprofitable and inconvenient. By holding wealth in the form of gold and bank notes which in themselves may be useless, the individual retains purchasing power which will be recognized

[306]

by his fellow citizens at any future time. Money acts as a store of value.

But as a human tool, money has more than these academic uses. It is more than a token and a yardstick. It is an active motivating force. It is a cause of definite results—one of the four causes, the efficient cause—about which Aristotle spoke. For instance, let us assume that a high minded millionaire bequeaths $5,000,000 for a school of business. Presto, a huge building comes into being, a faculty of learned men is assembled; catalogues giving publicity to the curriculum are formulated; students are attracted; a new vehicle for learning begins percolating its influence throughout the nation. The millionaire's mere thought of the new project, unsupported by his funds, might have been without effect. In a sense, the $5,000,000 was a cause of a significant development in education.

Money causes queer alignments. It directs the attention of gorgeous young women of the chorus to withered men of ancient vintage. It sometimes determines—usually with disastrous results—the course of sacred marriage. It lures pure scientists from priceless research to insignificant commercial pursuits. It sometimes turns zealous reporters into prejudiced propagandists. At its worst, it occasionally causes men in public office to betray the democracy which has honored them.

Money is a tool, not a passive instrument, but a radio-active one. Like other human instruments, it is capable of infinite abuse. The social utility of money depends upon the use to which it is put. And that hinges entirely upon the character of the individual who handles money.

All of the foregoing, baldly stated, seems the quintessence of the obvious. But whole nations have been ensnared into dangerous adventures through confused thinking about the inner nature of money. Because in certain countries the masses have not achieved full liberation and happiness under a money economy, the multitudes have sometimes vented their passions on this alleged root of all evil. Failing to create adequate substitutes, they have in a subsequent rule of chaos discovered that their action was similar to smashing a thermometer to end an unbearable spell of warm weather.

History relates many attempts to end popular unhappiness by destroying the very thing which the masses strive to obtain as a chief objective in life—money, free buying power. In ancient Rome, in the eighteenth century, in France at the time of the Revolution, and in America just before the adoption of the Constitution, unsuccessful efforts were made to

[308]

On the Alleged Root of All Evil

escape from the niggardliness of nature through unrestricted production of money tokens. Usually, after outbursts against money standards, periods of economic chaos follow, and then come times of slow restoration of the rule of sound money.

Perhaps money, supported by universally accepted gold metal, is a mere fetish unbacked by pure reason. But even if this is true, no other symbol has as yet been devised which serves society so effectively. Money is a crude, unstable tool, challenging improvement and betterment. But the human race in its muddling struggle toward progress, has frequently been retarded because heterodox leaders confused the weakening of money standards with general advances in the lot of the common man.

In the United States, which at this writing is the one important country in the world which adheres to the orthodox concept of a gold currency, substitutes play a more direct rôle in business than money itself. The bank check, which is an order that an individual with funds on deposit at a bank gives to the financial institution to pay a certain sum to another person, obviates the use of metal or paper currency and may be written to cover the precise amount of a given obligation, such as $1,007.18.

Currency is an ordinary paper substitute for money issued by a bank on a government's authority,

[309]

Common Sense of Money and Investments

or by the government itself. In the United States at present (as of May 1, 1924) the following types of money and currency are in use.

TABLE OF THE KINDS OF MONEY IN THE UNITED STATES [1]
AMOUNT OUTSTANDING

TYPE OF MONEY   (duplications in parentheses)   REMARKS

Gold coin and bullion
$4,417,401,937   Coinage of gold dollars discontinued in 1890. A dollar equals 25.8 grains; 90% fine. The real basis of the country's money. (Only $404,000,000 in actual circulation.)

Silver dollars
501,919,769   In ratio of 16:1 to silver dollars. Metallic content much less than face value.

Subsidiary silver
277,510,375   Metallic content less than face value.

TOTAL METALLIC:
$10,196,832,081

United States Notes
($1,428,026)   U. S. Government promises to pay face value on demand. Not secured nominally, but gold has been set aside to redeem them.

Federal Reserve Bank Notes
11,581,170   Issued by Federal Reserve Bank. Secured by 100% in U. S. government bonds.

Federal Reserve Notes
2,444,073,880   Issued by federal reserve agent. Se-

[1] From the U. S. Treasury Report of May, 1924.

[310]

On the Alleged Root of All Evil

cured by 40% in gold, 60% in commercial paper. Chief circulating medium of U. S. monetary system. Technically obligations of the government.

National Bank Notes
777,406,992 — Issued by national banks. Secured by equivalent face value of U. S. government bonds. Only bank notes before 1913.

TOTAL NOTES:
$3,224,490,068

Gold certificates
($1,140,199,279 for which gold is included above.) — Issued to represent one gold dollar in the treasury vaults, like warehouse receipts.

Silver certificates
406,898,667 — Issued to represent one silver dollar in the treasury vaults.

TOTAL REPRESENTATIVE PAPER MONEY: $1,547,097.896 AGGREGATE: (Eliminating reserves as duplications) $8,776,575,139 of which $4,760,113,559 is in circulation, or $42.33 *per capita*.

In addition, about $100,000,000 bronze one-cent pieces and nickel five-cent pieces.

Notions about money have changed little since the time of Aristotle. The Greek philosopher properly regarded money as altogether different from wealth which he looked upon as the sum of useful things of which money was only a symbol. Aristotle thought of money almost exclusively as a medium of exchange. This stream of thought continued through the middle ages, and was articulated by scholastic thinkers such as Thomas Aquinas (in Summa Theo-

[311]

logica) and later by Adam Smith and the early classical economists of the last century. Their views are sometimes known as the supply and demand theory, which held that money gave concrete form to economic demand.

A second theory espoused by John Stuart Mill, and held by several leading economists in the United States, looks upon gold as a commodity and holds that its value is determined by economic laws just as that of all other goods is. This explanation is known as the marginal utility theory.

Since the time of David Ricardo, the cost of production theory of money has also held an honored place at the round tables of economists. It contends that a unit of money is worth the cost of labor and materials of producing $1.00 or unit of gold. It is favored by the Austrian school of economic writers and by J. Lawrence Laughlin in this country at the present time.

Vogues in ideas change even as cycles in modes and manners. A fourth theory, the quantity theory of money, is now the most popular among economists. It holds that the purchasing power of money is determined by the amount outstanding in relation to all goods available for sale. In other words, the more money there is the less it is worth. The opposition party among the economists asserts that the quantity theory is meaningless. B. M. Anderson, Jr., an American economist who is one of the leaders in this camp, asserts that money has many more than the four conventional uses specified, and that each contributes to its "absolute social value." One of the most important of these is the desire to gain money because of its social prestige, which raises its value.

The seemingly endless production of paper money in Europe after the Great War, resulting in a riot of inflation and a ruthless disturbance of money standards, requires special mention. The value of paper money having no security behind it is determined chiefly by expectations of ultimate redemption in gold at a certain rate and is hence considered an exception to the quantity theory. Money in such circumstances is a defaulted promise to pay gold.

To the layman, academic theories about money have little significance. He takes money for granted, regarding it as natural as the atmosphere that surrounds him. The ordinary individual is likely to err, however, when he forgets that money is simply a convenient tool, not an ultimate goal.

CHAPTER XXXII

BOOKS AS STEPPING STONES TO BUSINESS SUCCESS

A Bibliography of Informative Volumes.

To no better purpose can you elevate your spare hours than to study economic questions.—ANDREW CARNEGIE.

BOOKS are compensation for our limited allotment of time in which to live and achieve.

They are instruments of economy, making it possible for the ordinary individual with restricted opportunities to experiment, to draw on the best of all human experience through the ages.

In recent decades business has become infinitely more complex. A revolution of industrial and commercial methods has gradually increased the demand for scientifically trained men in the factories, in the sales offices and in the counting rooms. Scores of universities have in recent years formulated schools of higher education for business executives.

Although the rush of students to the universities is unprecedented and overtaxes available facilities, the proportion of those who enter the college classroom is extraordinarily small in comparison with those who learn the business of life under their own guidance through trial and error in the office, in the factory, or on the farm.

Yet, desirable as well divided university training is, the colleges have no exclusive ownership of knowledge. The individual with initiative can perpetually increase his command over the facts of life while earning a living, in spite of the new complexities.

Business has ceased to be looked upon as a lowly pursuit for the vulgar. Having attained a new dignity, it is no longer apologetic. In recent years the workaday world has tended to become scientific. The great money reservoirs—the banks—and the huge instruments of production and distribution,— the modern corporations—have taken on staffs of economists who relate the specific activities of the money making institutions to the main streams of human enterprise and thinking.

In the last two decades a vast and unprecedented array of literature about contemporary barter has sprung into being. Tomes, profound and superficial, on every aspect of the American nation's pastime of money-getting have been written. Practitioners and philosophers have rushed into print to express in systematic form the hows and the wherefores of present day finance and trade. Instead of

[315]

the elementary exchanges of the middle ages, business in this age of intense specialization, has become an immensely complex mechanism, highly differentiated, and in its larger significance somewhat obscure and enigmatic to the masses who man its machinery.

Perhaps more books on business in all its phases have already been written than anyone can read. Some of the recent creations in the field of economic literature are excellent in style and in content. Many others are written in a technical language, which would elude the grasp of the ordinary man and woman. Others are replete with inner problems of trade of no importance to the outsider. Some are trivial and of transient interest. The layman, seeking to find his way through the ever increasing mass production of books on every subject from floorwalking to the art and science of managing a peanut stand, needs an experienced guide to lead him from the less important to the more significant works.

Much wisdom and experience are embodied in the literature of the subject. Yet business is a living thing, perpetually changing and offering the highest rewards to those of creative minds who are resilient and resourceful. Books can reinforce native intelligence by buttressing it with the facts, but cannot supply the spark of intelligence itself.

[316]

BIBLIOGRAPHY

GIVING A LIST OF THE BEST BOOKS ON EACH OF THE MAJOR SUBJECTS TREATED IN THE FOREGOING CHAPTERS FOR THOSE WHO SEEK FURTHER INFORMATION:

CHAPTER	SUBJECT	BOOK	AUTHOR
1	Money	The Purchasing Power of Money	Irving Fisher
		Money and Banking	Horace White
		The Meaning of Money	Hartley Withers
		The Principles of Money	J. Lawrence Laughlin
		Money and Banking	J. T. Holdsworth
2 and 3	Thrift	The New Thrift	Bolton Hall
		How to Get Ahead	Albert W. Atwood
		Thrift	Harry J. Lewis
		Training in Thrift	Eleanor R. Larrison
		Saving and Investing Money	Thomas E. Saunders
4 and 5 7, 8, 9 and 10	Investment and Speculation	Principles of Bond Investment	Lawrence Chamberlain
		Financial Organization and Management	Charles W. Gerstenberg
		The Stock and Produce Exchanges	Albert W. Atwood
		Investment and Speculation	Thomas Conway

[317]

Bibliography

		Scientific Stock Speculation	Charles H. Dow
		Stocks and Shares	Hartley Withers
		Railroad Securities	A. A. Sakolski
		Investment Analysis	W. E. Lagerquist
		Speculation	S. S. Huebner
		Bonds and Stocks	Roger W. Babson
6	The Radical and his Bonds	New Worlds for Old	H. G. Wells
11	Switching Investments	How to Invest When Prices are Rising	Irving Fisher and others
		High Prices and Deflation	E. Walter Kemmerer
12 13 and 14	Brokers	Course of Study for Brokerage, Stock Exchange, Investment Banking	Robert L. Smitley
		Business of Finance	Hartley Withers
		Funds and Their Uses	Frederick A. Cleveland
15	Stock Exchanges	The Work of the Stock Exchange	J. Edward Meeker
		The Stock Market	S. S. Huebner
		The Stock Exchange from Within	Wm. E. Van Antwerp
16	Opportunities	The Genius of American Business	Julius H. Barnes
17	Insurance	Life Insurance	S. S. Huebner
		Principles of Insurance	W. F. Gephart

Bibliography

20	Accounting	Accounting Theory and Practice	Roy B. Kester
21	Forecasting	Business Barometers	Roger Babson
		Business Cycles	Wesley C. Mitchell and others
		Business Forecasting	David F. Jordan
		Business and Investing Forecasting	Ray Vance
24	Captains of Industry	Men Who Are Making America	B. C. Forbes
26	Credit Unions	A Credit Union Primer	A. H. Ham
		Coöperative Credit Societies	E. L. Whitney
27	Instalments	Credits and Collections	Skinner & White
28	Household Budgeting	Economics of the Household	B. R. Andrews
		Successful Family Life on the Small Income	May H. Abel
29	Job Picking	Personnel Relations in Industry	A. M. Simons
		Management and Men	Meyer Bloomfield
		Selection of Employes	Ernest A. Edkins
30	Old Age Retirement	Poverty and Waste	Hartley Withers

[319]

GLOSSARY

of financial terms in every-day use not fully defined elsewhere in this volume.

ACCRUED INTEREST—To prices paid for bonds, the amount of interest which has accumulated since the last semi-annual interest date, which is the accrued interest, must be added.

ANNUITY— A fixed income or allowance received in one or more payments each year.

ARBITRAGE—Simultaneous buying of a security or commodity in one market and selling in another market to take advantage of a difference in price.

ASKED PRICE—The price at which a security or commodity is offered for sale.

ASSETS—Property of all sorts belonging to an individual or corporation.

ASSESSMENT—A call upon stockholders to pay into the treasury of the company a certain sum per share.

BABY BOND—A bond certificate of $500, $100 or less at face value.

BANKRUPTCY—The inability of a corporation to pay a fixed legal debt, payment of which is formally demanded by the creditor.

BEAR—A speculator who believes prices will decline.

BID—The price which a buyer is willing to pay for a security or commodity.

BOND—An interest bearing obligation to pay money.

[320]

Glossary

BOOKS CLOSE—Relates to the stock transfer record books of a company. On the day fixed for the closing of the books, only those entered as stockholders on that day are considered such, regardless of changes taking place thereafter through purchase or sale of the stock, and are entitled to dividends or voting power, for which the books close.

BOOKS OPEN—The opening of the stock transfer books, usually same days after the closing, permits transfer of shares on the books of the company.

BULL—A speculator who believes prices will rise.

CALL—An option to buy stock at or before a fixed future date and at a fixed price.

CALL MONEY—Loans secured by readily marketable securities and payable on demand of the lender on 24 hours notice.

CALLED BOND—Bonds called for redemption at a fixed date, after which interest ceases.

CAPITALIZATION—Securities representing the value of a business.

CHEAP MONEY—Relates to the plentifulness of money available for borrowing, as shown by low interest rates.

CLOSING PRICE—The final price at which a security sells on a given day.

COLLATERAL—Security pledged for the payment of an obligation.

COMMISSION—A fee payable to a broker for the execution of an order.

CONSOL—Perpetual interest bearing obligations of the British government (originally "consolidated annuities").

CONSORTIUM—An international combination of nations or financiers to help finance another nation.

[321]

Glossary

CONVERSION—Exchange of one issue of securities for another issue.

CONVERTIBLE PRICE—The rate at which the conversion may be made.

CORNER—A situation in the market for a stock when all purchasable shares are held by one interest, who can then advance the price at will. It is accentuated when speculators who have sold the stock short find they are unable to repurchase it.

CURB—A security market place outside the leading exchange.

DEFLATION—An economic process of business and financial contraction, marked by falling commodity and security prices and reduced commercial and industrial activity.

EQUITY—The margin of value possessed by a security in a property over and above prior claims, such as mortgages, etc.

EX-DIVIDEND—Without declared dividends.

EX-RIGHTS—Without the privilege to participate in new stock subscriptions or any other privilege that might have been granted by a corporation to its stockholders.

FISCAL YEAR—The twelve months counted as a year by a nation or corporation in its financial operations.

FLAT—Without interest.

FORECLOSURE—A legal procedure to apply the security to the payment of a defaulted secured debt.

FROZEN ASSETS—Assets not convertible into cash over a long period.

FUNDED DEBT—Obligations evidenced by bonds or notes.

GRAIN PIT—A place in the Chicago Board of Trade where brokers in grain meet to transact business.

Glossary

HEAVY MARKET—A term used to indicate a slackening of demand and easing off of prices.

HEDGING—An operation intended as a protection against loss in another operation.

HYPOTHECATION—A pledge of security for a loan, giving the broker or bank the right to sell upon default of payment.

INFLATION—An economic process of business and financial expansion, marked by rising prices and increasing activity, opposite of deflation.

INVENTORY—Stock of grade on hand.

LETTER OF CREDIT—An advice addressed by banks to agents or correspondents to pay a specific person certain sums on demand, for which they assume responsibility.

LIABILITIES—Something owed. All debts or obligations to pay money or its equivalent.

LIEN—A legal right to hold a specified property until a pecuniary claim against the owner has been satisfied.

LIQUIDATION—Payment of a loan or claim; or conversion of securities into cash; or winding up of the affairs of an enterprise.

LISTED SECURITIES—Having the privilege of being dealt in on an organized exchange.

LOAN CROWD—The gathering of brokers on the New York Stock Exchange who desire to borrow or lend stocks.

MARGIN—The percentage of the price of a security bought by a speculative holder to protect his broker against possible loss.

MORTGAGE—A legal transfer of title to property which becomes effective only in case borrower does not pay off his debt as agreed.

[323]

Glossary

MONEY MARKET—A general term for transactions relating to money, such as banks and brokerage, loans, discounts, etc.

MONEY RATES—Rates of interest currently paid for loans of various types.

NEGOTIABLE—Title passing by delivery.

OLD LOT—A block of fewer than 100 shares of stock; or less than $1,000 in bonds.

PAR VALUE—The nominal or stated value of a security, as printed on its face.

POOL—A combination of speculators to achieve a desired manipulation.

PUT—A contract calling upon the issuer to buy stock named in the agreement within a specified period at a fixed price, at the option of the purchaser of the put.

REALIZE—To reduce property to cash; or obtain a profit from an operation by winding it up.

REDISCOUNT RATE—The rate of interest charged for discounting a note or acceptance that has already been discounted once.

RELOADING—A device used by questionable security venders to sell additional shares of stock in the same or an allied company to individuals who have already fallen for their wares.

RENTES—Perpetual French government bonds.

REORGANIZATION—The readjustment in the financial affairs of a bankrupt corporation which permits the removal of the receiver.

RESERVE RATIO—In bank statements, the percentage relation of reserves to liabilities.

RIGHTS—A privilege given stockholders of a corporation

to subscribe to new securities on specified terms, evidenced by certificates, usually negotiable.

SCRIP—Certificates representing fractions of shares, usually carrying no dividend or voting rights but convertible into full shares when presented to the company in amounts equal to the face value of one or more shares.

SHORT SALE—The sale of a security not possessed, but borrowed, in the hope of being able to purchase later at a lower figure.

SPECIALTY—A stock representing a company not engaged in a standard industry, such as railroading, steel, oil, etc.

STRADDLE—A combined put and call, giving the holder an option to either buy or sell at a fixed price within a given period.

SYNDICATE—A group of capitalists or bankers acting together for a single purpose, such as underwriting a new security issue.

TAPE—The strip of white paper on which the ticker prints quotations.

TIME MONEY—Money borrowed or loaned for a fixed period.

UNDERWRITER—Individual, bank or syndicate guaranteeing to furnish the money needed in a particular transaction.

UNLOADING—A Wall Street term for general selling of stock by their holders, usually by pool manipulators or those close to the management of corporations.

UPSET PRICE—The minimum price at which the court will permit property to be sold at a receivership sale following foreclosure.

Glossary

WHIPSAWED—A Wall Street colloquialism, meaning a speculator has sustained a double loss in first buying and then selling short, or vice versa.

BOND YIELDS

To find the precise yield, yield books, based on logarithms, are required. To find the approximate yield, divide the closing quotation on a bond into the rate of annual return. If the bond is selling below par, you must allow also for the appreciation of the principal. To do this, subtract the market quotation from par, or 100, and divide the remainder by the number of years the bond has to run before maturity.

For example, if a 6 per cent bond is selling at 90 and has ten years to run, the annual return will be 6.66 per cent. The difference between par and the market price will be 10 points, subtracting 90 from 100. Dividing ten points by ten years, the quotient will be 1. This figure is to be added to 6.66, which is the annual return, and the result, 7.66 per cent, will give you the approximate yield.

The yield of a bond selling at a premium may be found by the same principles. If a 6 per cent bond sells at 110 and has ten years to run, the annual return is found to be 5.5 per cent on the purchase price. The premium of ten points, divided by the ten years the bond is to run, gives a quotient of 1. This figure is to be subtracted from 5.5, the annual return, and the result, 4.5 per cent, is the appromixate yield.

BOND INTEREST TABLE

INTEREST ON $1,000

On the Basis of 360 Days to the Year—30 Days for 1 Month

The bond interest table is useful primarily in determining the interest due on bonds bought or sold between interest dates, and on account balances with brokers. The annual rate of income table on the next page will reveal the return on dividend paying stocks if the current price and annual dividend are known.

	3%	3½%	3¾%	4%	4¼%	4½%	4¾%	5%
1 Day	0.0833	0.0972	0.1042	0.1111	0.1181	0.1250	0.1319	0.1389
1 Month	2.5000	2.9167	3.1250	3.3333	3.5416	3.750	3.9583	4.1667
2 Months ...	5.0000	5.8333	6.2500	6.6667	7.0833	7.5000	7.9167	8.3333
3 Months ...	7.5000	8.7500	9.3750	10.0000	10.6250	11.2500	11.8750	12.5000
6 Months ...	15.0000	17.5000	18.7500	20.0000	21.2500	22.5000	23.7500	25.0000

	5¼%	5½%	5¾%	6%	6¼%	7%	7½%	8%
I Day	0.1458	0.1528	0.1597	0.1667	0.1806	0.1944	0.2083	0.2222
1 Month	4.3750	4.5833	4.7917	5.0000	5.4167	5.8333	6.2500	6.6666
2 Months ...	8.7500	9.1667	9.5833	10.0000	10.8333	11.6666	12.5000	13.3333
3 Months ...	13.1250	13.7500	14.3750	15.0000	16.2500	17.5000	18.7500	20.0000
6 Months ...	26.2500	27.5000	28.7500	30.0000	32.5000	35.0000	37.5000	40.0000

Glossary

ACTUAL RATE OF INCOME

On Dividend Paying Stocks at Various Prices

Price %	2%	3%	4%	5%	6%	7%	8%
20	10.0	15.0	20.0	25.0	30.0	35.0	40.0
21	9.5	14.3	19.1	23.8	28.6	33.3	38.1
22	9.1	13.6	18.2	22.7	27.3	31.8	36.4
23	8.7	13.0	17.4	21.7	26.1	30.4	34.8
24	8.3	12.5	16.7	20.8	25.0	29.2	33.3
25	8.0	12.0	16.0	20.0	24.0	28.0	32.0
26	7.7	11.5	15.4	19.2	23.1	26.9	30.8
27	7.4	11.1	14.8	18.5	22.2	25.9	29.6
28	7.1	10.7	14.3	17.9	21.4	25.0	28.6
29	6.9	10.3	13.8	17.2	20.7	24.1	27.6
30	6.7	10.0	13.3	16.7	20.0	23.3	26.7
31	6.5	9.7	12.9	16.1	19.4	22.6	25.8
32	6.3	9.4	12.5	15.6	18.8	21.9	25.0
33	6.1	9.1	12.1	15.2	18.2	21.2	24.2
34	5.9	8.8	11.8	14.7	17.7	20.6	23.5
35	5.7	8.6	11.4	14.3	17.1	20.0	22.9
36	5.6	8.3	11.1	13.9	16.7	19.4	22.2
37	5.4	8.1	10.8	13.5	16.2	18.9	21.6
38	5.3	7.9	10.5	13.2	15.8	18.4	21.1
39	5.1	7.7	10.3	12.8	15.4	18.0	20.5
40	5.0	7.5	10.0	12.5	15.0	17.5	20.0
41	4.9	7.3	9.8	12.2	14.6	17.1	19.5
42	4.8	7.1	9.5	11.9	14.3	16.7	19.1
43	4.7	7.0	9.3	11.6	14.0	16.3	18.6
44	4.6	6.8	9.1	11.4	13.6	15.9	18.2
45	4.4	6.7	8.9	11.1	13.3	15.6	17.8
46	4.4	6.5	8.7	10.9	13.0	15.2	17.4
47	4.3	6.4	8.5	10.6	12.8	14.9	17.0
48	4.2	6.3	8.3	10.4	12.5	14.6	16.7
49	4.1	6.1	8.2	10.2	12.2	14.3	16.3
50	4.0	6.0	8.0	10.0	12.0	14.0	16.0
51	3.9	5.9	7.8	9.8	11.8	13.7	15.7
52	3.9	5.8	7.7	9.6	11.5	13.5	15.4
53	3.8	5.7	7.6	9.4	11.3	13.2	15.1
54	3.7	5.6	7.4	9.3	11.1	13.0	14.8
55	3.6	5.5	7.3	9.1	10.9	12.7	14.6
56	3.6	5.4	7.1	8.9	10.7	12.5	14.3
57	3.5	5.3	7.0	8.8	10.5	12.3	14.0
58	3.5	5.2	6.9	8.6	10.3	12.1	13.8
59	3.4	5.1	6.8	8.5	10.2	11.9	13.6
60	3.3	5.0	6.7	8.3	10.0	11.7	13.3
61	3.3	4.9	6.6	8.2	9.8	11.5	13.1
62	3.2	4.8	6.5	8.1	9.7	11.3	12.9
63	3.2	4.8	6.4	7.9	9.5	11.1	12.7
64	3.1	4.7	6.3	7.8	9.4	10.9	12.5
65	3.1	4.6	6.2	7.7	9.2	10.8	12.3
66	3.0	4.6	6.1	7.6	9.1	10.6	12.1
67	3.0	4.5	6.0	7.5	9.0	10.5	11.9
68	2.9	4.4	5.9	7.4	8.8	10.3	11.8
69	2.9	4.4	5.8	7.3	8.7	10.1	11.6
70	2.9	4.3	5.7	7.1	8.6	10.0	11.4
71	2.8	4.2	5.6	7.0	8.5	9.9	11.3
72	2.8	4.2	5.6	6.9	8.3	9.7	11.1
73	2.7	4.1	5.5	6.9	8.2	9.6	11.0
74	2.7	4.1	5.4	6.8	8.1	9.5	10.8
75	2.7	4.0	5.3	6.7	8.0	9.3	10.7

Price %	4%	5%	6%	7%	8%	9%	10%
76	5.3	6.6	7.9	9.2	10.5	11.8	13.2
77	5.2	6.5	7.8	9.1	10.4	11.7	13.0
78	5.1	6.4	7.7	9.0	10.3	11.5	12.8
79	5.1	6.3	7.6	8.9	10.1	11.4	12.7
80	5.0	6.3	7.5	8.8	10.0	11.3	12.5
81	4.9	6.2	7.4	8.6	9.9	11.1	12.3
82	4.9	6.1	7.3	8.5	9.8	11.0	12.3
83	4.8	6.0	7.2	8.4	9.6	10.8	12.1
84	4.8	6.0	7.1	8.3	9.5	10.7	11.9
85	4.7	5.9	7.1	8.2	9.4	10.6	11.8
86	4.7	5.8	7.0	8.1	9.3	10.5	11.6
87	4.6	5.8	6.9	8.1	9.2	10.3	11.5
88	4.6	5.7	6.8	8.0	9.1	10.2	11.4
89	4.5	5.6	6.7	7.9	9.0	10.1	11.2
90	4.4	5.6	6.7	7.8	8.9	10.0	11.1
91	4.4	5.5	6.6	7.7	8.8	9.9	11.0
92	4.4	5.4	6.5	7.6	8.7	9.8	10.9
93	4.3	5.4	6.5	7.5	8.6	9.7	10.8
94	4.3	5.3	6.4	7.5	8.5	9.6	10.6
95	4.2	5.3	6.3	7.4	8.4	9.5	10.5
96	4.2	5.2	6.3	7.3	8.3	9.4	10.4
97	4.1	5.2	6.2	7.2	8.3	9.3	10.3
98	4.1	5.1	6.1	7.1	8.2	9.2	10.2
99	4.0	5.1	6.1	7.1	8.1	9.1	10.1
100	4.0	5.0	6.0	7.0	8.0	9.0	10.0
101	4.0	5.0	5.9	6.9	7.9	8.9	9.9
102	3.9	4.9	5.9	6.9	7.8	8.8	9.8
103	3.9	4.9	5.8	6.8	7.8	8.7	9.7
104	3.9	4.8	5.8	6.7	7.7	8.7	9.6
105	3.8	4.8	5.7	6.7	7.6	8.6	9.5
106	3.8	4.7	5.7	6.6	7.6	8.5	9.4
107	3.7	4.7	5.6	6.5	7.5	8.4	9.3
108	3.7	4.6	5.6	6.5	7.4	8.3	9.3
109	3.7	4.6	5.5	6.4	7.3	8.3	9.2
110	3.6	4.6	5.5	6.4	7.3	8.2	9.1
111	3.6	4.5	5.4	6.3	7.2	8.1	9.0
112	3.6	4.5	5.4	6.3	7.1	8.0	8.9
113	3.5	4.4	5.3	6.2	7.1	8.0	8.9
114	3.5	4.4	5.3	6.1	7.0	7.9	8.8
115	3.5	4.4	5.2	6.1	7.0	7.8	8.7
116	3.5	4.3	5.2	6.0	6.9	7.8	8.6
117	3.4	4.3	5.1	6.0	6.8	7.7	8.6
118	3.4	4.2	5.	5.9	6.8	7.6	8.5
119	3.4	4.2	5.0	5.9	6.7	7.6	8.4
120	3.3	4.2	5.0	5.8	6.7	7.5	8.3
125	3.2	4.0	4.8	5.6	6.4	7.2	8.0
130	3.1	3.9	4.6	5.4	6.2	6.9	7.7
135	3.0	3.7	4.4	5.2	5.9	6.7	7.4
140	2.9	3.6	4.3	5.0	5.7	6.4	7.1
145	2.8	3.5	4.1	4.8	5.5	6.2	6.9
150	2.7	3.3	4.0	4.7	5.3	6.0	6.7
155	2.6	3.2	3.9	4.5	5.2	5.8	6.5
160	2.5	3.1	3.8	4.4	5.0	5.6	6.0
165	2.4	3.0	3.6	4.2	4.8	5.5	6.3
170	2.4	2.9	3.5	4.1	4.7	5.3	5.1
175	2.3	2.9	3.4	4.0	4.6	5.1	5.9
180	2.2	2.8	3.3	3.9	4.4	5.0	5.7
190	2.1	2.6	3.2	3.7	4.2	4.7	5.6
200	2.0	2.5	3.0	3.5	4.0	4.5	5.2

INDEX

For definitions only, see glossary.

Index

[330]

Index

[331]

Index

Index